Scala Functional Programming Patterns

Grok and perform effective functional programming in Scala

Atul S.Khot

BIRMINGHAM - MUMBAI

Scala Functional Programming Patterns

First published: December 2015

Production reference: 1181215

Published by Packt Publishing Ltd.
Livery Place
35 Livery Street
Birmingham B3 2PB, UK.

ISBN 978-1-78398-584-5

www.packtpub.com

Credits

Author
Atul S. Khot

Reviewers
Subhajit Datta
Rui Gonçalves
Zahidul Islam
Steve Perkins
Hawk Weisman

Commissioning Editor
Julian Ursell

Acquisition Editor
Nikhil Karkal

Content Development Editor
Divij Kotian

Technical Editor
Pranjali Mistry

Copy Editor
Neha Vyas

Project Coordinator
Nikhil Nair

Proofreader
Safis Editing

Indexer
Monica Ajmera Mehta

Graphics
Disha Haria

Production Coordinator
Arvindkumar Gupta

Cover Work
Arvindkumar Gupta

About the Author

Atul S. Khot learned programming by reading C code and figuring out how it works. From there, he moved on to writing a lot of C++ code and then moved further to Java and Scala. He is an avid open source advocate who loves scripting languages and clean coding. He is ever ready to learn a new command-line trick. Atul currently works at Webonise Labs, Pune. He was also a panelist for Dr. Dobb's Jolt Awards. Last but not least, he is a trekking enthusiast and also a big foodie.

Aknowledgement

A big thanks to my late mother, Sushila S. Khot. Aai, you taught me human values. You were a teacher all your life, and felt very deeply for young girls and their education. I remember those countless occasions when you helped needy girls with school supplies. You gave so much to the blind school and countless others. Looking back, I feel so proud that you never differentiated between me and my sisters. I will always be human, my dear mother, and will never let you down. I know in my heart of hearts that you are just a prayer away!

A big thanks to my late father, Shriniwas V. Khot. Anna, to me you will always be a hero who fought for a free and united India. I learned from you that freedom is invaluable and life is not meant to be easy. Always a fierce fighter all your life, you wanted me to stand up for what's right and just. You always encouraged me to take the road less traveled. You are no more, but there are so many cherished moments. Memories keep flooding back and I marvel at what gem of a father I had! You will always live on in my memories!

I want to deeply thank the technical reviewers of this book, Rui Gonçalves, Steve Perkins, Hawk Weisman, Zahidul Islam, and Shubhajit. I was continually amazed by the depth of knowledge and insight your feedback carried. Needless to say, I learned a lot from you all. It was simply great working with you all—y'all rock!

Hearthfelt thanks to the wonderful Scala community for all the support. I am continually amazed by the spirit to help budding Scala programmers!

A special mention of my draft reviewer and editor, Divij Kotian. He has a super sharp eye for detail, immense dedication, and has been a pillar of strength. In addition to the meticulous reviews, Divij also coordinated all the review and publishing phases. Divij you are a gem—you know your stuff!

A special thanks to Pranjali, Joanna, and Neha. I am continually amazed by all your attention to detail in making sure that the book is error free. I feel privileged working with you! Ever indebted.

Big thanks to Nikhil Karkal! Nikhil, you got us all together and gave me the opportunity to work with all these amazing people. Without your support and help, this book would not have been possible. Big thanks! You are the best!

Last but not least, thanks to my wife, Rupali. It is comforting to know you are there always! And to Kalyani, my daughter—my precious, thanks for keeping my hopes alive!

I would like to thank my colleagues at Webonise Lab for the wonderful environment, support, and understanding. Working with you all has been a privilege!

About the Reviewers

Rui Gonçalves is an all round hardworking and dedicated software engineer. He is an enthusiast of software architecture, programming paradigms, distributed systems, algorithms, and data structures. He loves learning new stuff everyday and working with state-of-the-art technologies. He loves the open source model and is an active contributor. He has the ambition of building products and services that have a great impact on society.

He currently works at ShiftForward, where he is a software engineer in the online advertising field. He is focused on designing and implementing highly efficient, concurrent, and scalable systems working in tandem with machine learning solutions. In order to achieve this, he uses Scala as his main development language on a day-to-day basis.

Steve Perkins is the author of *Hibernate Search by Example* and has over 15 years of experience working with enterprise Java. He lives in Atlanta, GA, USA, with his wife, Amanda, and their children, Drew and Katie. Steve currently works as an architect at BetterCloud, where he writes software for Google Apps, Microsoft Office 365, and other cloud platforms.

When he is not writing code, Steve plays plays fiddle and guitar and enjoys working with music production software. You can visit his technical blog at `steveperkins.com` and follow him on Twitter at `@stevedperkins`.

Md Zahidul Islam is a software engineer working in a reporting team at Confirmit, Inc. He specializes in stream processing, Apache Spark, and Scala.

He has a passion for large-scale distributed computing infrastructure (Hadoop), messaging systems (RabbitMQ, Kafka), NoSQL databases (HBase, Cassandra, MongoDB), and functional programing. He has also reviewed *Scala for Machine Learning*, which is an excellent book on machine learning.

Currently, he is developing data-driven product features for reporting tools. Earlier in his career, he worked with C#, ASP.NET, Web API, and everything around the .NET ecosystem.

You can read his blog at `http://zahidul-islam.com` and follow him at @zahidsharp or contact him directly at `zahidsharp@outlook.com`.

I would like to thank my wife, Sandra, who lovingly supports me in everything I do. I'd also like to thank Packt Publishing and its staff for giving me the opportunity to contribute to this book.

www.PacktPub.com

Support files, eBooks, discount offers, and more

For support files and downloads related to your book, please visit www.PacktPub.com.

Did you know that Packt offers eBook versions of every book published, with PDF and ePub files available? You can upgrade to the eBook version at www.PacktPub.com and as a print book customer, you are entitled to a discount on the eBook copy. Get in touch with us at service@packtpub.com for more details.

At www.PacktPub.com, you can also read a collection of free technical articles, sign up for a range of free newsletters and receive exclusive discounts and offers on Packt books and eBooks.

https://www2.packtpub.com/books/subscription/packtlib

Do you need instant solutions to your IT questions? PacktLib is Packt's online digital book library. Here, you can search, access, and read Packt's entire library of books.

Why subscribe?

- Fully searchable across every book published by Packt
- Copy and paste, print, and bookmark content
- On demand and accessible via a web browser

Free access for Packt account holders

If you have an account with Packt at www.PacktPub.com, you can use this to access PacktLib today and view 9 entirely free books. Simply use your login credentials for immediate access.

Table of Contents

Preface

This is a book on functional programming patterns using Scala. Functional programming uses functions as basic building blocks. These are functions that don't have any side effects. This challenges our notions about how to write programs. The order of execution for such functions does not matter. We get to reason about them in a referentially transparent manner. This can be a big help in proving correctness. It feels just like a plain arithmetic problem, where (2+2)*(3+3) always equals 24. You may evaluate the expression as 2+2 first, or as 3+3.

I got to know about the Unix culture early in my career. The Unix philosophy relies on pipelining small programs, each doing functionally one and only one thing. One can connect these processing nuggets together. In addition to these hundreds of ready-made building blocks, you could write your own too. These could be easily connected in the pipeline. These pipes and filters were a deeply influential concept as a whole. When I saw Scala's combinators, options, and for comprehensions, I knew I was looking at pipes and filters again. The nuggets in this case were Scala functions instead of Unix processes. Understanding functional programming gives you a new perspective on your code and programming in general. The other aspect of pipelining is that you tend to reuse them intuitively, and you also write less. Though you iterate lines of a text file in a Unix shell pipeline, you don't write any for loops. These are done for you. You just specify which lines pass your criteria or how to transform these lines or both.

Scala allows you to do just that—albeit in a somewhat different form. You don't need to write a for loop, and you keep away from loop counters. Instead, the language invites you to write for comprehensions. Immutability is an actively advocated rule of thumb. Another is avoiding side effects. Scala advocates both. As you probably know, immutability paves the way for more robust concurrency. Why are these so important? Simple, we need to reason about code. Any strategy that makes this activity controlled and simpler is a godsend! Does going down the immutable route mean we end up doing too much copying? How would this Copy On Write measure up against large data structures? Scala has an answer for this in the form of structural sharing.

One-liners are very popular as they get a lot done in a line of code. Scala features allow you to compose such one-liners. Instead of reiterating the same collection, you can do it in one elegant expression. For example, creating an immutable class with constructor and equality comparison defined that is bestowed with destructuring powers is just a one-liner. We just define a case class. There are many situations where Scala one-liners save a lot of programmer time and result in far less code. Combinators such as map, flatMap, filter, and foreach are composed together to express a lot of logic in a one-liner. How does it all affect a program design and design patterns? Here are a few illustrative cases. The singleton design pattern is used to ensure that only one instance of a class could ever exist. Null Objects are specialized singletons that are used to avoid nulls and null checks. Scala's Options give us a similar functionality. Scala's object keyword gives us ready-made singletons. Singletons are specialized factories. A factory creates objects. Scala's syntactic sugar give us a very succinct way to use the apply factory method.

The command design pattern encapsulates an object as a command. It invokes a method on the object. Scala has parameters by name. These are not evaluated at the call site but instead are evaluated at each use within the function. This feature effectively replaces the command pattern with first-class language support. The strategy pattern encapsulates algorithms and allows us to select one at runtime. In Java, we could express the strategy as an interface and the varying algorithms as concrete implementations. Scala's functions are first-class objects. You can pass functions around as method arguments and return values. Functions can be very effective substitutes for the strategy pattern. The ability to define anonymous functions is really helpful here. The Decorator pattern is needed at times. It can be used to decorate (that is, extend) the functionality of an object without modifying it. Some design plumbing needs to be done though. Scala's stackable traits can express the same design very elegantly. One use of the proxy design pattern is for implementing lazy evaluation. When some computation is expensive, we do it only when needed.

As we are very familiar with eager evaluations, we create a list in memory and think it is fully realized. However, just like eager lists, there are lazy lists too. If we think of a typical OR (| |) conditional statement, if the left operand is true, the right is not evaluated. This is a very powerful concept. Scala's streams provide lazy lists.

Chain of responsibility is another handy pattern that is used to decouple the sender of a request from its receiver and allows more than one object (a chain of objects) to handle a request. If any object in the chain is not able to handle the request, it passes the request to its next object in the chain. Scala's partial functions fit this bill nicely. We can chain partial functions with Scala's orElse operator to realize the pattern. When we write code, we need to handle errors. Scala's Try/Success/Failure again allows us to write pipelines, and if any piece of the pipeline is an error, rest of the pipeline processing is skipped.

We will look at all these concepts in greater detail. We will set up a problem, look at the traditional Java solution, and then see how Scala changes the game.

Welcome to the Scala wonderland!

What this book covers

Chapter 1, Grokking the Functional Way, gives you an eagle's eye view of functional programming and its advantages: succinct and readable code. Also, this chapter compares the command pattern in Java and Scala.

Chapter 2, Singletons, Factories, and Builders, covers singletons and Null Objects as specialized singletons. Scala Options are null objects. This also covers Scala's support for factory method and builders.

Chapter 3, Recursion and Chasing Your Own Tail, discusses the concept of recursion and Scala's support for it. It also looks at how recursion advocates immutability and the concept of structural sharing.

Chapter 4, Lazy Sequences – Being Lazy, Being Good, talks about eager versus lazy evaluation and the proxy design pattern. It also talks about Scala's streams and infinite lists.

Chapter 5, Taming Multiple Inheritance with Traits, covers Scala traits, mix-ins, and stackable modifications. It also covers dependency injection and the Cake pattern.

Chapter 6, Currying Favors with Your Code, covers lexical scope, closures, partially applied functions, and currying. This chapter also discusses the loan pattern, template method pattern, and another way to implement decorators.

Chapter 7, Of Visitors and Chains of Responsibilities, covers the Visitor pattern and its application. The other topics that are discussed are Scala's pattern matching capabilities and the chain of responsibility pattern. We will also learn Scala implementation using orElse and the collect idiom.

Chapter 8, Traversals – Mapping/Filtering/Folding/Reducing, covers iterators and functional iteration using map, filter, fold, and reduce. This chapter introduces Monads and explains ReduceLeft and ReduceRight.

Chapter 9, Higher Order Functions, discusses the strategy pattern and Scala version using higher order functions. It covers map as a functor, flatMap as a Monad, and foldLeft as Monoids. Here, you will also learn how to iterate lazy collections.

Chapter 10, Actors and Message Passing, showcases a case study to recursively grep a directory for files that contain matching text. It also covers the producer consumer pattern and the Master Slave pattern. It explains the concept of poison pills, event-driven programming, immutability, and concurrency. It also talks about Akka and Actors and how to reimplement recursive grep using Actors.

Chapter 11, It's a Paradigm Shift, teaches you how to sort in Scala and the Schwarzian transform implemented in Scala. It discusses functional error handling with Try/Success/Failure. And talks about Java Threads versus Scala's Futures. Scala's Parser Combinators are also discussed here.

What you need for this book

You would need Scala installed — a version greater than or equal to 2.11. I refer to pipelining a lot, so it would be pretty helpful if you are trying out the examples on Linux or Mac. You can use cygwin too if it is a Windows box you are running.

Version 0.13 of the sbt tool (http://www.scala-sbt.org/) will also be needed.

A typical Java dev environment is assumed too. The examples are tested with Maven version 3 and JDK 8.

Who this book is for

We assume that you have written Java code for a while. You also should have a basic knowledge of Scala. A knowledge of Java and Scala fundamentals is assumed. Familiarity with basic data structures such as binary trees and linked lists is assumed.

This is a text about patterns and design ideas that you can use again and again. A basic understanding of design patterns would be great. I have explained the problem and the patterns and the typical object-oriented Java solution. The Scala solution builds on top of all this know-how. The text also assumes that you have written some multithreaded Java code. I have explained the necessary concepts, but haven't explained multithreading from the ground up.

Most of the concepts are explained and pointers are provided for further reading.

Conventions

In this book, you will find a number of text styles that distinguish between different kinds of information. Here are some examples of these styles and an explanation of their meaning.

Code words in text, database table names, folder names, filenames, file extensions, pathnames, dummy URLs, user input, and Twitter handles are shown as follows: "We can include other contexts through the use of the `include` directive."

A block of code is set as follows:

```
// Driver code
public static void main(String[] args) {
    Driver c = new Driver();
SomeInterface c1 = c.create(10); // 2
    SomeInterface c2 = c.create(20); // 3

 c1.printMsg(); // prints 10
c2.printMsg(); // prints 20
 }
```

Any command-line input or output is written as follows:

```
scala> def f(n: Int) = {
     |    val k = (y: Int) => y < n // 1
     |    k
     | }
f: (n: Int)Int => Boolean
```

New terms and **important words** are shown in bold. Words that you see on the screen, for example, in menus or dialog boxes, appear in the text like this: "Clicking the **Next** button moves you to the next screen."

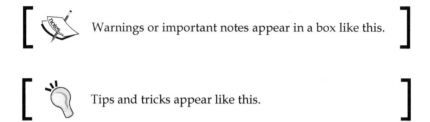

Warnings or important notes appear in a box like this.

Tips and tricks appear like this.

Reader feedback

Feedback from our readers is always welcome. Let us know what you think about this book—what you liked or disliked. Reader feedback is important for us as it helps us develop titles that you will really get the most out of.

To send us general feedback, simply e-mail feedback@packtpub.com, and mention the book's title in the subject of your message.

If there is a topic that you have expertise in and you are interested in either writing or contributing to a book, see our author guide at www.packtpub.com/authors.

Customer support

Now that you are the proud owner of a Packt book, we have a number of things to help you to get the most from your purchase.

Downloading the example code

You can download the example code files from your account at http://www.packtpub.com for all the Packt Publishing books you have purchased. If you purchased this book elsewhere, you can visit http://www.packtpub.com/support and register to have the files e-mailed directly to you

Errata

Although we have taken every care to ensure the accuracy of our content, mistakes do happen. If you find a mistake in one of our books—maybe a mistake in the text or the code—we would be grateful if you could report this to us. By doing so, you can save other readers from frustration and help us improve subsequent versions of this book. If you find any errata, please report them by visiting http://www.packtpub. com/submit-errata, selecting your book, clicking on the Errata Submission Form link, and entering the details of your errata. Once your errata are verified, your submission will be accepted and the errata will be uploaded to our website or added to any list of existing errata under the Errata section of that title.

To view the previously submitted errata, go to https://www.packtpub.com/books/ content/support and enter the name of the book in the search field. The required information will appear under the Errata section.

Piracy

Piracy of copyrighted material on the Internet is an ongoing problem across all media. At Packt, we take the protection of our copyright and licenses very seriously. If you come across any illegal copies of our works in any form on the Internet, please provide us with the location address or website name immediately so that we can pursue a remedy.

Please contact us at copyright@packtpub.com with a link to the suspected pirated material.

We appreciate your help in protecting our authors and our ability to bring you valuable content.

Questions

If you have a problem with any aspect of this book, you can contact us at questions@packtpub.com, and we will do our best to address the problem.

1
Grokking the Functional Way

Before we start learning Scala, let's first understand what **functional programming** (**FP**) is. You may have used a spreadsheet while working. In a spreadsheet, there is a bunch of equations and we enter values in the given cells for these equations. We get the answers through these equations. When you enter the same values again, you get the same answer and there are no fallouts.

At the core of FP is composition. Looking at a software system made up of parts, we build bigger parts by composing smaller parts. If you think about it, most complex systems are composed of parts, which in turn are composed of smaller parts. Functional languages give us the means to make this composition. One of the prominent functional languages that can be used for FP is **Scala**.

Scala in Italian means a staircase. If you look at the language's logo, you will see it's a staircase. The language acts as a staircase through which we can ascend and become better at programming. Scala also refers to the very many techniques that we can use to control the complexity of large-scale systems.

We will begin to learn Scala by looking at abstractions. We will see why abstractions are good and how Scala helps us to be abstract. Scala code is concise and expressive. A lot of the concise expression is due to functions. Functions are an important pillar of functional programming. In this chapter, we will look at pure and impure functions. Reducing the number of moving parts to be used is an effective technique to control programming complexity. Immutability is another pillar of FP that helps us here. To see all this in effect, we will take a problem example and implement the solution in Java. Then, we will solve the problem using Scala. Looking at a few Scala one-liners will help us to get started with **READ/EVALUATE/PRINT LOOP** (**REPL**). We will use Scala REPL extensively throughout the entire book.

Finally, we will look at idioms and patterns. Traditional patterns in Scala look very different from their Java counterparts. We will briefly look at the command and strategy of Scala and see how functions are used to pass algorithms around.

Welcome to the Scala fun ride!

Abstractions

What do we mean by abstractions? Why are they important? To understand this, we will compare two approaches. First, the "go to the wall and pull at one of the wooden panels fitted into the rectangular hole" approach versus the "open the door, please" approach.

A door is an abstraction. We really don't care whether it is made of wood or some other material, or what type of a lock it has, or any other details. The details are important, but not always. If we worry about the details always, we would quickly get bogged down, and all the communication would effectively come to a halt.

A table is an abstraction, so is a chair, and so is a house. I hope you get the drift. We want to be *selectively ignorant of the details at times*, and selective ignorance is **abstraction**.

Now, you may ask why does it matter to us programmers? The reason is that it gets things done in a compact manner.

For example, let's look at the following Scala code, which is used to count the frequency of characters in a string:

```scala
scala> "hello world".toList.filter(_.isLetter).groupBy(x => x).map { y =>
     |    y._1 -> y._2.size
     | }
res1: scala.collection.immutable.Map[Char,Int] = Map(e -> 1, l -> 3, h ->
1, r -> 1, w -> 1, o -> 2, d -> 1)
```

Isn't it compact?

On the Urban Dictionary website, http://www.urbandictionary.com/define. php?term=cutie, the term "cutie" is defined as compact beauty — the kind you just want to put in your pocket and keep beside you forever.

I was bowled over when I first saw it all. It is concise, short, packs a punch, and is elegant. The **Type Less Do More** philosophy. Gets a lot done with less...

To run the code snippet, fire up the Scala REPL. This looks a lot like a command console, a prompt waiting for you to key in Scala code. In a command terminal, typing just Scala fires up the REPL:

~> scala

It will give the following output:

```
Welcome to Scala version 2.11.7 (Java HotSpot(TM)
64-Bit Server VM, Java 1.8.0_25).
```

You can type in expressions to have them evaluated and type help for more information. Let's try the following simple one line commands:

```
scala> 1 + 1
res2: Int = 2
scala> "hello".length
res4: Int = 5
```

For me, Scala brought the thrill back to programming... You can do a great deal by writing a few lines of code—less is more...

Scala gives you many tools, so the code is abstract and reusable...

Concise expression

You always want to be able to concisely express yourself. Let's try the following command to create a string:

```
scala> val list = List("One", "two", "three", "Four", "five")
list: List[String] = List(One, two, three, Four, five)
```

We have created a list of strings. Note that we neither had to specify the type of the list for this, nor any new keyword. We just expressed that we wanted a list assigned to a read-only variable.

Code reviews do a lot of good to a code base. I keep looking for places where I can replace a variable assignment with variable initialization. Refer to the following URL for an example: http://www.refactoring.com/catalog/replaceAssignmentWithInitialization.html.

Scala helps us with the `val` keyword. With the use of this keyword, we can establish the following:

- The initial value of variable must be specified (it is impossible for the variable to remain uninitialized).
- The value of variable cannot ever be changed again (there is one less moving part).

Why is this so important? A system with less moving parts is easier to understand and explain. You will be knowing that Google is well known for its less-moving-parts software. Let's try the following command to check for the uppercase in these characters:

```scala
scala> def hasUpperCaseChar(s: String) = s.exists(_.isUpper)
hasLowerCaseChar: (s: String)Boolean
```

What does `s.exists(_.isUpper)` do? In this code, I have a string and I am checking whether it has one or more uppercase characters.

Note that I need to look at each character of the string to arrive at an answer as output. However, I did not have to split the string into its constituent characters and then work on each character.

I am just expressing the algorithm. The algorithm involves iterating all characters. However, I did not write a loop. Instead, I expressed what I meant, concisely. Scala's strings are collections of characters. We can try the following command to make use of a filter method:

```scala
scala> list filter (hasUpperCaseChar)
res2: List[String] = List(One, Four)
```

Just like a string, `List` is again a collection, in this case, of strings. I used a list method, `filter`, to weed out elements that did not satisfy the predicate.

If we were to write this imperatively, we would need a nested loop (a loop within another loop). The first loop would take each string, and the inner loop would work on each character of the string. We would need a list to collect the matching elements.

Instead of lists, we just declared what we wanted to happen. However, at some point of time in the code the looping needs to happen! It does happen indeed, but behind the scenes and in the `filter` method.

The `filter` method is a higher order function that receives the `hasUpperCaseChar` function.

Let's say, in addition to this method, we want only those string elements that have a length greater than 3:

```scala
scala> list filter (x => hasLowerCaseChar(x) && x.size > 3)
res1: List[String] = List(Four)
```

We are again executing the algorithm; however, with a different match criteria. We are passing a function in the form of a function literal. Each element in the list is bound to x, and we run a check on x.

The preceding form of expression allows us to concisely express our intent. A large part of this flexibility comes from the idea of sending small computations around that are expressible without much ado. Welcome to functions!

Functions

Functional programming includes a lot about functions. There are different kinds of functions in programming, for example, pure functions. A pure function depends only on its input to compute the output. Let's try the following example to make use of functions:

```scala
scala> val addThem = (x: Int, y: Int) => x + y + 1
addThem: (Int, Int) => Int = <function2>
scala> addThem(3,4)
res2: Int = 8
```

As long as the function lives, it will always give the result 8 given the input (3, 4). Take a look at the following example of a pure function:

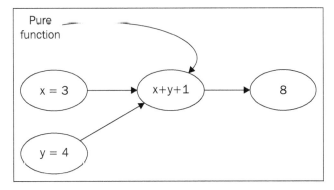

Figure 1.1: Pure functions

The functions worked on the input and produced the output, without changing any state. What does the phrase "did not change any state" mean? Here is an example of a not-so-pure function:

```scala
scala> var p = 1
p: Int = 1
scala> val addP = (x: Int, y: Int) => {
     |  p += 1
     |  x + y + p
     |  }
addP: (Int, Int) => Int = <function2>

scala> addP(3, 4)
res4: Int = 9
scala> addP(3, 4)
res5: Int = 10
```

This addP function changes the world — this means that it affects its surroundings. In this case, the variable p. Here is the diagrammatic representation for the preceding code:

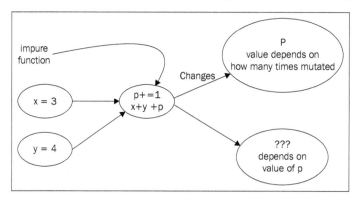

Figure 1.2 : An impure function

Comparing addThem and addP, which of the two is clearer to reason about? Remember that while debugging, we look for the trouble spot, and we wish to find it quickly. Once found, we can fix the problem quickly and keep things moving.

For the pure function, we can take a paper and pen, and since we know that it is **side effects free**, we can write the following:

```
addThem(3, 4) = 8

        addThem(1,1) = 3

        ...
```

For small numbers, we can do the function computation in our heads. We can even replace the function call with the value:

```
scala> addThem(1,1) + addThem(3,4)
res10: Int = 11
scala> 3 + 8
res11: Int = 11
```

Both the preceding expressions are equivalent. When we replace the function, we deal with **referentially transparent** expressions. If the function is a long running one, we could call it just once and cache the results. The cached results would be used for the second and subsequent calls.

The `addP` function, on the other hand, is referentially opaque.

Immutable

Each one of us has a name. Let's keep this simple — a first and last name. My first name is Atul and my last name is Khot. If someone suddenly called me by the name Prakash, things won't work!

Keeping aside cases such as writers taking a pen name (that is, Plum for PG Wodehouse), commonly each one of us has a standard, official name. We simply don't want parts of it changed to willy nilly. Let's try the following example:

```
scala> case class FullName(firstName: String, lastName: String)
defined class FullName
scala> val name = FullName("Bertie", "Wooster")
name: FullName = FullName(Bertie,Wooster)

scala> name.firstName = "Mrs. Bertie"
<console>:13: error: reassignment to val
        name.firstName = "Albert"

```

Scala stopped us changing the code of Woosters!! It just saved Bertie from getting a wife!

In case you need a break and some light relief, Google *The Code of the Woosters!*

Once a case class instance is created, it is sealed. You can read it, but you cannot change it:

```scala
scala> name.firstName
res12: String = Bertie
scala> name.lastName
res13: String = Wooster
```

You can even look at the signified version of the instance that the compiler writes for you:

```scala
scala> name
res14: FullName = FullName(Bertie,Wooster)
```

And you can destructure it using pattern matching. Immutability just reduces the moving parts and helps us to restore sanity. This is a boon when threads enter the picture.

Referential transparency

To understand referential transparency, let's first consider the following description:

Let me tell you a bit about India's capital, New Delhi. The Indian capital houses the Indian Parliament. The Indian capital is also home to Gali Paranthe Wali, where you get to eat the famous parathas.

We can also say the following instead:

Let me tell you a bit about India's capital, New Delhi. New Delhi houses the Indian Parliament. New Delhi is also home to Gali Paranthe Wali, where you get to eat the famous parathas.

Here, we substituted New Delhi with the Indian capital, but the meaning did not change. This is how we would generally express ourselves.

The description is referentially transparent with the following commands:

```scala
scala> def f1(x: Int, y: Int) = x * y
f1: (x: Int, y: Int)Int

scala> def f(x: Int, y: Int, p: Int, q: Int) = x * y + p * q
f: (x: Int, y: Int, p: Int, q: Int)Int

scala> f(2, 3, 4, 5)
res0: Int = 26
```

If we rewrite the `f` method as follows, the meaning won't change:

```
scala> def f(x: Int, y: Int, p: Int, q: Int)= f1(x, y) + f1(p, q)
f: (x: Int, y: Int, p: Int, q: Int)Int
```

The `f1` method just depends upon its arguments, that is, it is pure.

Which method is not referentially transparent? Before we look at an example, let's look at Scala's `ListBuffer` function:

```
scala> import scala.collection.mutable.ListBuffer
import scala.collection.mutable.ListBuffer
```

The `ListBuffer` is a mutable collection. You can append a value to the buffer and modify it in place:

```
scala> val v = ListBuffer.empty[String]
v: scala.collection.mutable.ListBuffer[String] = ListBuffer()

scala> v += "hello"
res10: v.type = ListBuffer(hello)

scala> v
res11: scala.collection.mutable.ListBuffer[String] = ListBuffer(hello)

scala> v += "world"
res12: v.type = ListBuffer(hello, world)

scala> v
res13: scala.collection.mutable.ListBuffer[String] = ListBuffer(hello,
world)
```

Armed with this knowledge, let's now look at the following command:

```
scala> val lb = ListBuffer(1, 2)
lb: scala.collection.mutable.ListBuffer[Int] = ListBuffer(1, 2)

scala> val x = lb += 9
x: lb.type = ListBuffer(1, 2, 9)
scala> println(x.mkString("-"))
```

```
1-2-9

scala> println(x.mkString("-"))

1-2-9
```

However, by substituting x with the expression (lb += 9), we get the following:

```
scala> println((lb += 9).mkString("-")) // 1
1-2-9-9
scala> println((lb += 9).mkString("-")) // 2

1-2-9-9-9
```

This substitution gave us different results. The += method of ListBuffer is not a pure function as there is a side effect that occurred. The value of the lb variable at 1 and 2 is not the same.

The problem – grouping continuous integers

A while back, I wanted a simple and elegant way to solve the following problem:

Given: A sorted list of numbers

When: We group these numbers

Then: Each number in a group is higher by one than its predecessor. So, let's be good and write a few tests first:

```
@Test
public void testFourGroup() {
  List<Integer> list = Lists.newArrayList(1, 2, 3, 4, 5, 9, 11,
    20, 21, 22);
  List<List<Integer>> groups = groupThem.groupThem(list);
  assertThat(groups.size(), equalTo(4));
  assertThat(groups.get(0), contains(1, 2, 3, 4, 5));
  assertThat(groups.get(1), contains(9));
  assertThat(groups.get(2), contains(11));
  assertThat(groups.get(3), contains(20, 21, 22));
}
@Test
public void testNoGroup() {
  List<Integer> emptyList = Lists.newArrayList();
  List<List<Integer>> groups = groupThem.groupThem(emptyList,
```

```
    new MyPredicate());
  assertThat(groups, emptyIterable());
}
@Test
public void testOnlyOneGroup() {
  List<Integer> list = Lists.newArrayList(1);
  List<List<Integer>> groups = groupThem.groupThem(list,
    new MyPredicate());
  assertThat(groups.size(), equalTo(1));
  assertThat(groups.get(0), contains(1));
}
```

We will make use of the excellent Hamcrest matchers (and the excellent Guava library) to help us express succinctly what we want our code to do.

Java code

You know the drill! Let's roll up our sleeves and dish out some code. The following looks pretty good:

```
public List<List<Integer>> groupThem(final List<Integer> list) {
  final List<Integer> inputList =
    Colletions.unmodifiableList(list);
  final List<List<Integer>> result = Lists.newArrayList();
  int i = 0;
   while( i < inputlist.size()){
   i = pickUpNextGroup(i, inputList, result); // i must progress
   }
 return result;
 }

 private int pickUpNextGroup(final int start, final
  List<Integer> inputList,
    final List<List<Integer>> result) {
  Validate.isTrue(!inputList.isEmpty(),
    "Input list should have at least one element");
  Validate.isTrue(start <= inputList.size(), "Invalid start
    index");

  final List<Integer> group = Lists.newArrayList();

  int currElem = inputList.get(start );
```

```
group.add(currElem); // We will have at least one element
    in the group

int next = start + 1; // next index may be out of range

while (next < inputList.size()) {
  final int nextElem = inputList.get(next); // next is in range
  if (nextElem - currElem == 1) { // grouping condition
   group.add(nextElem);
   currElem = nextElem; // setup for next iteration
  } else {
   break; // this group is done
  }
  ++next;
}
result.add(group); // add the group to result list
Validate.isTrue(next > start); // make sure we keep moving
return next; // next index to start iterating from
            // could be past the last valid index
}
```

This code has a lot of subtlety. We use the Apache commons 3 validation API for asserting the invariants. Download this book's source code to check out the unit test.

We are using the excellent Guava library to work with lists. Note the ease of this library, with which we can create and populate the list in one line. Refer to `https://code.google.com/p/guava-libraries/wiki/CollectionUtilitiesExplained` for more details.

We are careful to first make the input list an **unmodifiable list** — to protect ourselves from stepping on our toes... We also need to carefully arrange the iteration to make sure that it eventually terminates and we do not accidentally access a non-existent list index (try to say it without gulping).

Going scalaish

Remember the sermon on being abstract? Our Java code is dealing with a lot of higher level and lower level details — all at the same time... We really don't want to do that; we wish to selectively ignore the details... We really don't want to deal with all the corner cases of iteration — the Java code is worried stiff about looking at two consecutive elements and the corner cases.

What if this was somehow handled for us so we can focus on the business at hand? Let's take a look at the following example:

```scala
def groupNumbers(list: List[Int]) = {
  def groupThem(lst: List[Int], acc: List[Int]): List[List[Int]] = lst
match {
    case Nil => acc.reverse :: Nil
    case x :: xs =>
      acc match {
        case Nil => groupThem(xs, x :: acc)
        case y :: ys if (x - y == 1) =>



        case _ =>
            acc.reverse :: groupThem(xs, x :: List())
      }
  }
  groupThem(list, List())
}
groupNumbers(x)
```

Thinking recursively...

This version looks a lot better—doesn't it? We use features such as nested functions and recursion and get stuff such as immutability for free... A list in Scala is immutable.In Java, we need to work a bit more to make things immutable. In Scala, it is the other way around. You need to go a little further to bring in mutability... We also use something called persistent data structures that have nothing to do with databases here. We will look at it in detail in a while...

However, a bit better version follows—meaning a tail-recursive version. Take a look at the following example of it:

```scala
def groupNumbers(list: List[Int])(f: (Int, Int) => Boolean) :
List[List[Int]] = {
  @tailrec
  def groupThem(lst: List[Int], result: List[List[Int]], acc:
List[Int]): List[List[Int]] = lst match {
    case Nil => acc.reverse :: result
    case x :: xs =>
      acc match {
        case Nil => groupThem(xs, result, x :: acc)
```

```
            case y :: ys if (x - y == 1) =>

                groupThem(xs, result, x :: acc)

        case _ =>
                groupThem(xs, acc.reverse :: result, x :: List())
        }
    }
    val r = groupThem(list, List(), List())
    r.reverse
}
```

The `@tailrec` function does some good to our code. This is an annotation that we put on a method. We use it to make sure that the method will be compiled with **tail call optimization (TCO)**. TCO converts the recursive form into a loop.

If the Scala compiler cannot apply TCO, it flags an error. Recursion and TCO are covered in detail in *Chapter 3, Recursion and Chasing Your Own Tail*.

Now, having set the stage—let's look at the reusability feature...

Reusability – the commonality/variability analysis

Instead of a fixed grouping criteria, could we make the Java version more dynamic? Instead of the expressing the condition directly in the code, we could wrap up the condition as a predicate:

```
if (nextElem - currElem == 1) { // grouping condition
```

A predicate is a function that returns a Boolean value. It should take two numbers and tell whether the predicate is `true` or `false`?

Now there could be multiple predicates. For example, we might want to find elements that differ by 2 or 3 numbers. We can define an interface as follows:

```
public interface Predicate {
        boolean apply(int nextElem, int currElem);
}

public class MyPredicate implements Predicate {

    public boolean apply(int nextElem, int currElem) {
        return nextElem - currElem == 1;
    }
}
```

Why would we do this? We would do this for two reasons:

- We would want to reuse the algorithm correctly and pick up two consecutive elements. This algorithm would handle all corner cases as in the previous cases.

- The actual grouping criteria in our case is `nextElem - currElem == 1`, but we can reuse the previous code to regroup the numbers using another criteria.

Here is how grouping would look; I am just showing the changed code:

```
public List<List<Integer>> groupThem(List<Integer> list, Predicate
myPredicate) {
    ...
        while (int i = 0; i < inputList.size();) {
            i = pickUpNextGroup(i, inputList, myPredicate, result); //
i must
            // progress
            ...
        }
}


private int pickUpNextGroup(int start, List<Integer> inputList,
Predicate myPredicate,
        List<List<Integer>> result) {
    ...
    final int nextElem = inputList.get(next); // next is in range
    // if (nextElem - currElem == 1) { // grouping condition
    if (myPredicate.apply(nextElem, currElem)) { // grouping condition
        group.add(nextElem);
    ...
    }
}
```

It is some work to define and use the predicate. Scala makes expressing this variability pretty easy, as we can use functions. Just pass on your criteria as a function and you are good to go:

```
def groupNumbers(list: List[Int])(f: (Int, Int) => Boolean) :  // 1 = {
  def groupThem(lst: List[Int], acc: List[Int]): List[List[Int]] = lst
match {
    case Nil => acc.reverse :: Nil
    case x :: xs =>
      acc match {
        case Nil => groupThem(xs, x :: acc)
```

```
         case y :: ys if (f(y, x)) =>
              // 2
              groupThem(xs, x :: acc)


    case _ =>
              acc.reverse :: groupThem(xs, x :: List())

         }

    }

  groupThem(list, List())

}
val p = groupNumbers(x) _  // 3
p((x, y) => y - x == 1)    // 4
p((x, y) => y - x == 2)    // 5
```

In 1, we use the function - `(f: (Int, Int) => Boolean)`.

The `f: (Int, Int) => Boolean` syntax means that f is a function parameter. The function takes two `Int` params and returns `Boolean`. Here is a quick REPL session to understand this better:

```
scala> val x : (Int, Int) => Boolean = (x: Int, y: Int)
=> x > y
x: (Int, Int) => Boolean = <function2>
scala> x(3, 4)
res0: Boolean = false
scala> x(3, 2)
res1: Boolean = true
scala> :t x
(Int, Int) => Boolean
```

We are using the `t` feature of the REPL to look at the type of x.

This is a function — a bit of code we can pass around — that corresponds to the previous Java predicate snippet. It is a function that takes two integers and returns a Boolean.

(A function is in fact a class that mixes in a trait, `function2` in our case).

At 2, we use it. Now comes the fun part.

At 3, we hold on to everything else except the function. And at 4 and 5, we just pass different functions. It would be more correct to say that we use function literals. lo and behold — we get the answers right.

This code also shows some currying and partially applied functions in action... We cover both of these features in *Chapter 6, Currying Favors with Your code.*

The one-liner shockers

Have you heard this phrase anytime: it is just a one-liner! You see all the work done in a single line of code, it seems almost magical. The Unix shell thrives on these one-liners. For example:

```
seq 1 100 | paste -s -d '*' | bc
```

Phew! This single command line generates a sequence of numbers, 1 to 100, generates a multiplication expression from these, and feeds the same to bca calculator that does the actual multiplication.

Scala has a legion of these. Here is one applied to our problem by using scalaz library.

> To try the following snippet, you need to install the scalaz library. It is not part of the Scala standard library. Here are a few simple instructions to install it.
>
> Create a directory of your choice and switch to it. Next, download and install the **Simple Build Tool** (**sbt**) from `http://www.scala-sbt.org/download.html`.
>
> ```
> /Users/Atulkhot/TryScalaz> sbt
> [info] Set current project to tryscalaz (in build
> file:/Users/Atulkhot/TryScalaz/)
> > set scalaVersion := "2.11.7"
> ... // output elided
> > set libraryDependencies += "org.scalaz" %%
> "scalaz-core" % "7.1.0"
> ... // output elided
> > console
> ...
> ```

Now the following snippet should work after installing the scalaz library:

```scala
scala> import scalaz.syntax.std.list._
import scalaz.syntax.std.list._
scala> List(1, 2, 3, 4, 6, 8, 9) groupWhen ((x,y) => y - x == 1)
res3: List[scalaz.NonEmptyList[Int]] = List(NonEmptyList(1, 2, 3, 4),
  NonEmptyList(6), NonEmptyList(8, 9))
```

Using functions the solution is just a one-liner:

```scala
scala> List(1, 3, 4, 6, 8, 9) groupWhen ((x,y) => y - x == 2)
res4: List[scalaz.NonEmptyList[Int]] = List(NonEmptyList(1, 3),
NonEmptyList(4, 6, 8), NonEmptyList(9))
```

So we are just not writing any of the supporting code—just stating our criteria for grouping.

You can read more about Scalaz at `http://eed3si9n.com/learning-scalaz/`.

Scala idioms

When do we know a language? In English, when we say a penny for your thoughts, we are using an idiom. We can express ourselves more succinctly and natively using these. Beating around the bush is another one. If we pick up enough of these and hurl them around at times, this will makes us fluent.

It is almost the same with programming languages. You see a construct time and again and make use of notable features of a specific programming language. Here is a sample of idioms from a few prominent languages.

For example, here is an idiomatic Scala way to sum up two lists of numbers:

```scala
scala> val d1 = List(1, 2, 3, 4, 5)
d1: List[Int] = List(1, 2, 3, 4, 5)

scala> val d2 = List(11, 22, 33, 44, 55)
d2: List[Int] = List(11, 22, 33, 44, 55)

scala> (d1, d2).zipped map (_ + _)
res0: List[Int] = List(12, 24, 36, 48, 60)
```

We could do this in a roundabout way; however, note that your Scala colleagues would quickly comprehend what is happening. Try the following command:

```
scala> (1 to 100).map( _ * 2 ).filter(x => x % 3 == 0 && x % 4 == 0 && x
% 5 == 0)
res2: scala.collection.immutable.IndexedSeq[Int] = Vector(60, 120, 180)
```

For numbers from 1 to 100, we multiply each number by 2. We select those numbers that are divisible by 3, 4, and 5.

Here we are chaining method calls together. Each method returns a new value. The input is left unmodified. The intermediate values are threaded from call to call.

We could also write the preceding command as follows

```
scala> val l1 = 1 to 100
… // output elided
scala> val l2 = l1.map(_ * 2)
 … // output elided
scala> val l3 = l2.filter(x => x % 3 == 0 && x % 4 == 0 && x % 5 == 0)
l3: scala.collection.immutable.IndexedSeq[Int] = Vector(60, 120, 180)
```

However, the fluent API style is more idiomatic.

 You can learn more about fluent interfaces at `http://www.martinfowler.com/bliki/FluentInterface.html`.

People relate easily to idiomatic code. When we learn and use various Scala idioms, we will write code in the **Scala way**.

Patterns and those aha! moments

Patterns have more to do with a software design such as how to compose things together, the kind of design template to be used, and so on. They are a lot more about interactions between classes and objects. Patterns are design recipes, and they illustrate a solution to a recurring design problem. However, idioms are largely specific to a language and patterns are more general and at a higher level. Patterns are also mostly language independent.

You can (and usually do) implement the same design patterns in the language you are working with.

The command design pattern

The command design pattern encapsulates an object. It allows you to invoke a method on the object at a later point. For example, we are used to the following code line:

Given a Java object:

```
a.someMethod(arg1, arg2);
a.method1(arg1, arg2);
a.method2(arg3);
```

We expect the call `a.method1` to complete before the `a.method2` call starts. On the other hand, consider a real life situation.

Let's say you go to a restaurant, sit at a table, and order food. The waiter scribbles down the order on a piece of paper. This piece of paper then goes to the kitchen, someone cooks the food, and the food is served. It makes sense to prepare food for someone who ordered earlier, so your order is queued.

In the preceding paragraph, the piece of paper holds the details of your order. This is the command object. The preceding description also talks about a queue where the someone who cooks is the invoker—he puts things in motion as per your command. Add the `undo()` functionality and you have the essence of the command design pattern. Database transactions need to undo the commands on failure—the rollback semantics, for example.

Here is a simple first cut as example:

```
def command(i : Int) = println(s"---$i---")
def invokeIt(f : Int => Unit) = f(1)
invokeIt(command)
```

 The `def` method gets converted to a function. This is called an ETA expansion. We will soon be looking at the details.

This is a bit unpalatable though. I can possibly pass any function whatsoever and possibly wreak havoc. So, to constrain the things we can possibly pass on to the invoker, we take a bit of help from the compiler by typing the following commands:

```
scala> case class Command(f: Int => Unit)
defined class Command

scala> def invokeIt(i: Int, c: Command) = c.f(i)
```

```
invokeIt: (i: Int, c: Command)Unit

scala> def cmd1 = Command(x => println(s"**${x}**"))
cmd1: Command

scala> def cmd2 = Command(x => println(s"++++${x}++++"))
cmd2: Command

scala> invokeIt(3, cmd1)
**3**

scala> invokeIt(5, cmd2)
++++5++++
```

It is so terse.

The strategy design pattern

Strategy helps us to define a set of algorithms, encapsulates each step, and selects one as appropriate.

Oh boy! Here it is. We surely have used the `java.util.Comparator` strategy interface at times that allows us to vary the `compare` algorithm as we see fit so we can sort arrays at will. Let's try the following example:

```
    Integer[] arr = new Integer[] { 1, 3, 2, 4 };
Comparator<Integer> comparator = new Comparator<Integer>() {
 @Override
 public int compare(Integer x, Integer y) {
  return Integer.compare(y, x); // the strategy algorithm -
   // for reverse sorting
  }
};
Arrays.sort(arr, comparator);
System.out.println(Arrays.toString(arr));
```

Scala makes it a breeze by using these strategy... Type the following command to sort an array:

```
scala> List(3, 7, 5, 2).sortWith(_ < _)
res0: List[Int] = List(2, 3, 5, 7)
```

Passing algorithms around

We need this ability to plug in an algorithm as needed. When we start applying a strategy, we really try to apply the **Open/Closed principle (OCP)**. We don't touch the `sort` algorithm internals, that is, the sort implementation is closed for modification. However, by passing in a comparator, we can use the algorithm to sort objects of various classes that are open for extension.

This open for extension feature is realized very easily in Scala, as it allows us to pass functions around.

Here's another code snippet as an example of passing functions:

```scala
def addThem(a: Int, b: Int) = a + b // algorithm 1
def subtractThem(a: Int, b: Int) = a - b // algorithm 2
def multiplyThem(a: Int, b: Int) = a * b // algorithm 3


def execute(f: (Int, Int) => Int, x: Int, y: Int) = f(x, y)


println("Add: " + execute(addThem, 3, 4))
println("Subtract: " + execute(subtractThem, 3, 4))
println("Multiply: " + execute(multiplyThem, 3, 4))
```

Here, these various strategy algorithms are functions—no boilerplate. Imagine writing this in Java. This code is possible because in Scala, we can pass functions around as objects. Furthermore, we can use a method where a function is expected:

```scala
val divideThem = (x: Int, y: Int) => x / y
println("Divide: " + execute(divideThem, 11, 5))
```

Scala's functions are first-class objects, meaning they can be sent to a method and returned from a method, just like a number or string. The ability to pass functions to other functions is a very powerful concept. It is one of the major pillars of FP, as we will soon see.

Summary

Scala is expressive and rich with tools that help us to eliminate boilerplates. It allows us to concisely express the intention of programming. Functions help us reuse the common facilities, freeing us from coding them every time.

Pure functions are simpler to reason about, as there are lot less moving parts. We can think of them in terms of referential transparency. Impure functions are hard to reason with. We saw how making things immutable also helps in reducing these moving parts.

Idioms are what make us use a language effectively. This is true for programming languages. Scala is a feature-rich functional programming language. We got a bird's eye view of a few Scala features, such as recursion and functions.

Design patterns are a programmer's vocabulary. Scala gives us a fresh perspective of patterns, and we saw how the use of functions makes using design patterns so very easy in Scala.

We implemented the solution to a problem in Java and Scala. We saw how succinct and expressive the Scala code is compared to its Java counterpart.

We got our feet wet in the Scala land. Let's look at these features in detail and see how Scala makes programming cool and fun again. We will start with singleton and factories. Get, set, and go!

2
Singletons, Factories, and Builders

It may sound funny—and I may be stating the obvious—but everyone needs to be born at some point. Go ahead and have a good laugh at that. It is that obvious. Objects, too, need to be born at some point to do useful work. Objects have a lifetime as well. An object is constructed—and hopefully it does something useful before it eventually dies.

In Java we can see the object such as:

```
Point p = new Point(23, 94);
```

We know what is going on—an object of class point is created; its constructor-invoked p is a reference to this newly created object.

At times, we want explicit control of the object-creation process. There are times when we want to allow creation of only one instance of a class. Creational design patterns deal with object-creation mechanisms. Refer to https://sourcemaking. com/design_patterns/creational_patterns for more information on creational patterns.

Creational patterns help create objects in a manner suitable to the situation. Some expensive objects may need to be lazy-initialized. Refer to http://martinfowler. com/bliki/LazyInitialization.html for a very nice introduction to lazy initialization.

Scala provides some nifty ways for lazy initialization, as we will soon see.

We will first look at singletons and then Null Object, a specialized singleton, to avoid null checks. We will use our understanding to implement a set of numbers as a **Binary Search Tree (BST)**. Scala Options are an alternative to null check-based programming. We will rewrite the set implementation in Scala using Options. We will also look at how singletons work in Scala and related idioms.

The next pattern we will look at is factories. We will look at the Java version first and redo the solution in Scala. We will look at some related Scala idioms too.

Singletons – being one and only one

A singleton is a class of which only a single instance can exist. How do we prevent anyone from creating yet another instance? The solution is to make the constructor inaccessible. Here it is:

```
public class Singleton {
      // Eager initialization
   private static final Singleton instance = new Singleton(); // 1

   private Singleton() { // 2
   /* client code cannot create instance */
   }

      // Static factory method
   public static Singleton getInstance() { // 3
    return instance;
   }

// Driver code
public static void main(String[] args) {
  System.out.println(Singleton.getInstance());
  System.out.println(Singleton.getInstance());
  }
 }
```

Dissecting the code:

- At 1, the static initializer creates the instance—also the final keyword ensures that the instance cannot be redefined.
- At 2, the constructor access is private, so only the class methods can access it.
- At 3, the public factory method gives access to the client code.

If you run the Java program, you will see the same object reference printed twice.

A singleton has many forms. There is a null check version and a double-checked locking pattern version. The preceding version is a nicer way — it is the eager-initialized version though.

 There is a related pattern called **Monostate**. Refer to `http://www.objectmentor.com/resources/articles/SingletonAndMonostate.pdf` for more on this.

Null Objects – singletons in another garb

One popular form in which singletons are used is the **Null Object** pattern. Let's see what a Null Object is.

Java gives us the null reference to indicate a missing value. We are not supposed to call a method on it as there is no object. If, erroneously, we do, we are greeted with a **Null Pointer Exception (NPE)**. When we design methods to return nulls, the client code that calls the method needs to check assiduously. This is what a typical null check-based Java code looks like:

```
Point p = makeAPoint(); // a method that returns null in some
cases
if (p != null) { // the dreaded null check - onus is on us...
    // We are on sure grounds
}
```

The problem is that the onus term is on us to check for a reference being null. Every call to makeAPoint() needs to be checked, as shown earlier. This soon becomes tedious.

 The inventor of the null keyword called it his billion dollar mistake!!! Please see `http://www.infoq.com/presentations/Null-References-The-Billion-Dollar-Mistake-Tony-Hoare`.

What is the way out? How do we return missing values? Instead of returning null, return a Null Object. Why? The point being is that it is a kind of point and not a null reference. So no NPEs are ever possible.

Linked lists and trees are restricted forms of a graph. Trees have parent/child (and at times sibling) relationships and they don't contain cycles. Hence, trees are **Directed Acyclic Graphs (DAG)**. A tree needs to end somewhere, the nodes without any children. These are leaf nodes and they use null pointers to indicate termination.

However, instead of a null pointer, we can use a **sentinel node**. A sentinel node is like a train terminus, a special node in a linked list or a tree, indicating **termination**. It is used as an alternative over nulls. Sentinel nodes do not hold any meaningful data. The traversal algorithms are slightly modified, so when a sentinel node is hit, we know we are done.

For example, let's look at a BST, designed with a sentinel node instead of nulls. BSTs are a well-known data structure, the nodes arranged such that the parent value is greater than the left child and lesser than the right child. A BST can be used as a set.

A set is a collection of unique values. If we try inserting duplicate values, the values are discarded. For example:

```scala
scala> val s = Set(1, 1, 2, 3, 4, 4, 2, 3)
s: scala.collection.immutable.Set[Int] = Set(1, 2, 3, 4)
scala> println(s)
Set(1, 2, 3, 4)
scala> s + 4
res9: scala.collection.immutable.Set[Int] = Set(1, 2, 3, 4)
scala> s + 5
res10: scala.collection.immutable.Set[Int] = Set(5, 1, 2, 3, 4)
We have got a new set. The old set is still as before.
scala> s
res11: scala.collection.immutable.Set[Int] = Set(1, 2, 3, 4)
```

We consider how to implement a set of numbers using BSTs. Note the terminating sentinel node and both its left and right arms are pointing at itself. Here it is depicted pictorially:

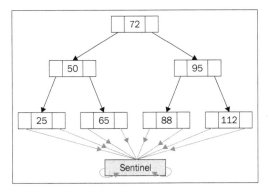

Figure 2.1: A Binary tree

First, an illustrative unit test; using those Hamcrest beauty matchers — the contains helper method is statically imported — makes sure our INORDER expectation is not violated.

The following test case adds some numbers — the insert call creates a tree. We performed an INORDER traversal on the BST. An INORDER traversal gets us the values in a sorted order:

```
package com.packt.chapter02;

import static org.hamcrest.Matchers.contains;
import static org.junit.Assert.assertThat;

import java.util.List;

import org.junit.Test;

import com.google.common.collect.Lists;

public class NodeTest {

  @Test
  public void testTraversal() {
   Node tree = Node.createTreeWithRoot(72);
     tree.insert(50);
     tree.insert(25);
     tree.insert(65);
     tree.insert(95);
     tree.insert(88);
```

```
        tree.insert(112);

    List<Integer> list = Lists.newArrayList();

    tree.traverseInOrder(list);

    assertThat(list, contains(25, 50, 65, 72, 88, 95, 112));
    }


    }
```

The implementation of the tree algorithms implements the tree data structure. The tree is terminated with a sentinel node. A **Node** is a binary search tree node. Our tree represents a set of numbers. Each tree node contains a number. The tree is formed by linking up child nodes. All values in the left sub-tree are less than the node value. Values in the right sub-tree are greater. We don't allow for duplicates as essentially our tree represents a set of numbers.

The sentinel node is represented by the nullNode. Note that it is never exposed to the outside world.

The Node class encapsulates the NullNode, which is a Null Object:

```
import java.util.List;

public class Node {

    private static final Node nullNode = new NullNode();
    private final int val;
    protected Node left;
    protected Node right;

    public Node(final int val) {
        this.val = val;
        this.left = nullNode;
        this.right = nullNode;
    }

    public void insert(final int i) {
        final Node node = new Node(i);
        insert(node);
    }

    ;

    public void insert(final Node n) {
```

```
        if (n.val < val) {
            left.insertLeft(n, this);
        } else if (n.val > val) {
            right.insertRight(n, this);
        }
        // else we found the value - do nothing, we
        // already have it
    }

    protected void insertLeft(final Node n, final Node
            parent) {
        insert(n);
    }

    protected void insertRight(final Node n, final Node
            parent) {
        insert(n);
    }

    public void traverseInOrder(final List<Integer> list) {
        left.traverseInOrder(list);
        list.add(val);
        right.traverseInOrder(list);
    }

    private static class NullNode extends Node {

        public NullNode() {
            super(Integer.MAX_VALUE); //
            this.left = this.right = this;
        }

        @Override
        public void traverseInOrder(final List<Integer>
                                                    list) {
            // do nothing
        }

        @Override
        protected void insertLeft(final Node n, final
        Node parent) {
            parent.left = n;  // Attach new node as
```

```
                        // left child of parent
                    }

                    @Override
                    protected void insertRight(final Node n, final
                    Node parent) {
                        parent.right = n; // Attach new node as right
                        // child of parent
                    }
                }


                // factory method to create the root node - and get
                // the ball rolling
                public static Node createTreeWithRoot(final int val) {
                    return new Node(val);
                }
            }
```

The big idea is to homogenize — a missing value is still a value, just a special value accessible only to the `Node` class, just like a singleton.

The `NullNode` is a Null Object. Look at the `traverseInOrder()` method of `NullNode`, it does nothing and so it terminates the recursion. We also override the `insertLeft(...)` and `insertRight(...)` methods — these just link up the child with its parent and thereby help grow the tree. Here it is depicted pictorially:

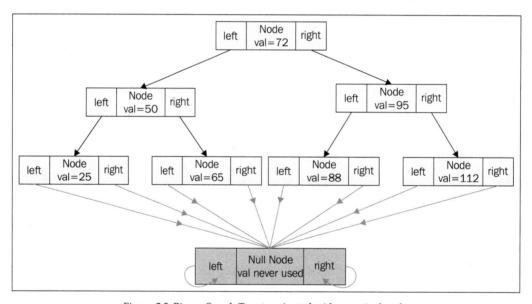

Figure 2.2: Binary Search Tree terminated with a sentinel node

How many `NullNodes` do you see? Note that our `NullNode` has no state of its own, it is a do nothing object—a place-holder! How many would we ever need? Just one would suffice! By design we only ever want one instance—we should prohibit creating more than one instance. Our null node is a singleton.

What value should the null node hold? Anything would do, as we don't use it. However, we must initialize it as it is final in the super class. We use the maximum number as a reminder to serve us that this is really a sentinel node. Its value does not have any business importance though.

Null Objects – the Scala way

Instead of using null to indicate missing values, Scala provides an `Option` class to represent optional values. `Option` can hold either `Some` value or `None` value. `None` indicates missing values. Please see `http://www.scala-lang.org/api/current/index.html#scala.Option`.

So instead of nulls, we return `None`. To see why, try the following code snippets in REPL:

```
scala> val m = List(Some("on"), None, Some("us"), None)

m: List[Option[String]] = List(Some(on), None, Some(us), None)
scala> for {

    |       Some(p) <- m

    | } println(p)

on

us

scala> val m = List(Some("on"), None, Some("us"), None)

m: List[Option[String]] = List(Some(on), None, Some(us), None)

scala> val p = m.flatten

p: List[String] = List(on, us)
```

See all the None getting filtered out? Let's continue further:

```
scala> val p = Some("one")

p: Some[String] = Some(one)

scala> val q = None

q: None.type = None

scala> val r = Option(null)

r: Option[Null] = None

scala> p.foreach(println(_)) // The _ is bound to the current element

one

scala> q.foreach(println(_))

scala> r.foreach(println(_))
```

How come the flatten and foreach calls are used with Options? These make sense for a container. For example, a List:

```
scala> val p = List(List(1,2), List(3,4))

p: List[List[Int]] = List(List(1, 2), List(3, 4))

scala> p.flatten

res0: List[Int] = List(1, 2, 3, 4)
```

Aha! These work for Options, too—as Options are containers holding zero or one object.

The map and flatMap operations are defined on Options. For Options holding one value that is. For a `Some`, these invoke the associated function. For a `None`, they do nothing. Let's check the following command lines:

```
scala> def m(n : Option[Int]) = n.map(_ + 1) // Options provide the map
operation
m: (n: Option[Int])Option[Int]

scala> val c1 = Some(10)
c1: Some[Int] = Some(10)

scala> val c2 = None
c2: None.type = None

scala> m(c1)
res19: Option[Int] = Some(11)

scala> m(c2)
res20: Option[Int] = None
```

So the map operation, when invoked over a `None`, simply did nothing:

```
scala> def m(n : Int) = if (n >= 0 && n < 10) Some(n) else None
m: (n: Int)Option[Int]
scala> m(10) foreach( x => println (x+1 ))
scala> m(5) foreach( x => println (x+1) )
```

The `foreach` increments and prints the number, if there is a Some. For a `None`, it does nothing.

Options are container

Let's put all this together to write the Scala version of the sentinel-based tree node. Let's first look at the picture:

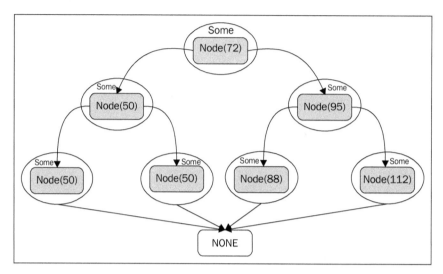

Figure 2.3: Option as Null Object

Here is the Scala code. (Note that our `TreeNode` is now a case class, with left and right fields as `Option[TreeNode]`. We also use `ListBuffer` instead of `List`):

```
object Tree extends App {

  case class TreeNode(v: Int, left: Option[TreeNode] = None,
                      right: Option[TreeNode] = None) {
    def add(av: Int) = {
      insert(av).get
    }

    def insert(av: Int): Option[TreeNode] = {
      def insertLeft(av: Int) =
        left.flatMap(_.insert(av)) orElse
          Option(TreeNode(av)) // 1

      def insertRight(av: Int) =
        right.flatMap(_.insert(av)) orElse
          Option(TreeNode(av)) // 2

      av.compare(v) match {
        case 0 => Option(this) // 3
```

```
      case -1 => Option(TreeNode(v, insertLeft(av),
        right)) // 4
      case 1 => Option(TreeNode(v, left, insertRight
        (av))) // 5
    }
  }
  def traverseItInOrder(): Option[List[TreeNode]] = {
    val leftList = left.flatMap(x => x
      .traverseItInOrder()).getOrElse(Nil)
    val rightList = right.flatMap(x => x
      .traverseItInOrder()). getOrElse(Nil)
    val result = (leftList :+ this) ++ rightList
    Option(result)
  }

  def traverseInOrder() = {
    val result: Option[List[TreeNode]] = traverseItInOrder()
    result.getOrElse(Nil)
  }
}

val p = TreeNode(4).add(3).add(0).add(1).add(99).
  add(1).add(4)

for {
  q <- p.traverseInOrder() // 5
} println(q.v)

}
```

Our `TreeNode` is a case class. The left and right child references are of type `Option[TreeNode]`. There is only one constructor that sets the left and right children to a `None`.

There is an `insert` method that we can use to add a value to the tree. As earlier, we check the argument and if it is less than this .val we try inserting it into the left arm otherwise in the right arm.

 The `left` can be either an `Some[TreeNode]` or None.

Let's try to understand the `flatMap` call:

```
left.flatMap(_.insert(av)) orElse Option(TreeNode(av))
```

This form uses infix notation for method invocation. What does it mean?

Scala provides a special invocation syntax when we have a method with one argument. The following method call:

```
o.m(arg)
```

can be written as:

```
o m arg
```

```
scala> val list = List.fill(5)(1) // we create a list of repeated 1
list: List[Int] = List(1, 1, 1, 1, 1)


scala> list.mkString("-") // invocation
res30: String = 1-1-1-1-1


scala> list mkString "-" // infix notation
res31: String = 1-1-1-1-1
```

Applying the same to our example:

```
scala> None.orElse(Some(10)) // invoking the orElse method on a None
res32: Option[Int] = Some(10)


scala> None orElse Some(10) // the infix notation
res33: Option[Int] = Some(10)


scala> Some(10) orElse Some(20)
res34: Option[Int] = Some(10)
```

Please see `http://docs.scala-lang.org/style/method-invocation.html`.

Let's try the following example:

```
scala> val left = None


left: None.type = None
```

```
scala> val right = Option("Hi")

right: Option[String] = Some(Hi)
scala> left orElse right
res7: Option[String] = Some(Hi)
```

In the `left.flatMap(_.insert(av))` expression, if `left` is `Some(TreeNode)` it reaches into the `Some`, which pulls out the `TreeNode` reference and invokes insert on it.

On the other hand, if `left` is `None`, the entire expression results in a `None` or else kicks into action—a new `TreeNode` is created and put into an `Option` and returned.

The salient points for the preceding code are as follows:

- Is symmetric—instead of left, it works on the right child reference.
- Works on the same principle—now for traversal, so if `left` is a `None`, nothing happens else we recursively traverse the left sub-tree.
- Same as case 2, if `right` is a `None`, nothing happens else we recursively traverse the right sub-tree.

Scala singletons

Scala has singleton objects called **companion objects**. A companion object is an object with the same name as a class. A companion object also can access private methods and fields of its companion class. Both a class and its companion object must be defined in the same source file. The companion object is where the `apply()` factory method may be defined. Let's have a look at the following example of a companion class:

```
class Singleton {   // Companion class
  def m() {
    println("class")
  }
}
```

And then its companion object as:

```
object Singleton { // Companion Object
  def m() {
    println("companion")
  }
}
```

It is that simple, when a case class is defined, Scala automatically generates a companion object for it.

The apply() factory method

If a companion object defines an `apply()` method, the Scala compiler calls it when it sees the class name followed by `()`. So, for example, when Scala sees something like:

$$Singleton(arg1, arg2, ..., argN) \text{ // syntactic sugar}$$

It translates the call into:

$$Singleton.apply(arg1, arg2,...,argN)$$

Open a Scala console and enter the following:

```
scala> val p = Map("one" -> 1, "two" -> 2)
p: scala.collection.immutable.Map[String,Int] = Map(one -> 1, two -> 2)
```

When we say `Map("one" -> 1, "two" -> 2)`, it seems like we are calling a function named `Map` with the arguments—however, this form is just syntactic sugar. Under the hood, `Map` has a companion object whose apply method is being called, then the `apply()` method creates the `Map` object and assigns it to `p`.

Every object can be called as a function, provided it has the `apply` method. For example, we can add an `apply` method ourselves and get the benefit of the syntactic sugar. The following uses REPL's `paste` mode. The `paste` mode, enabled via the `paste` command, allows you to enter multiline code snippets for evaluation:

```
scala> :paste
// Entering paste mode (ctrl-D to finish)
class C(x: Int) {
  def print() = println(x)
}
```

```
object C {
  def apply(n: Int) = {
    new C(n)
  }
}
```

press *Ctrl + D* here:

```
// Exiting paste mode, now interpreting.
defined class C
defined object C
scala> val k = C(9)
k: C = C@4b419a6b
scala> k.print()
9
```

The expression `C(9)` looks very much like a function call. As we see it is expanded to `C.apply(...)`.

Wait a minute! Does this apply to functions, too? Yes:

```
scala> val f = (l: List[Int]) => l.map(_ * 2)

f: List[Int] => List[Int] = <function1>

scala> f(List(1,2,3))

res0: List[Int] = List(2, 4, 6)
```

When we call `f(arg)` it gets translated to `f.apply(arg)`.

The factory method pattern

A factory method can further hide the actual concrete class implementing an interface. You have the factory method pattern, shown as follows:

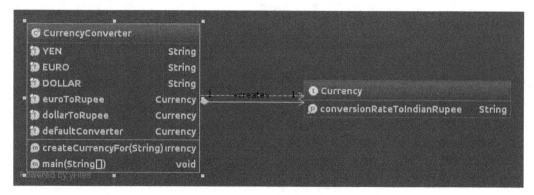

Figure 2.4: Factory Method UML

Also let's try the following program:

```java
public interface Currency {
 public String getConversionRateToIndianRupee();
}
public class CurrencyConverter {
 private static final String YEN = "Yen";
 private static final String EURO = "Euro";
 private static final String DOLLAR = "Dollar";

 private static final class EuroToRupee implements Currency {
  @Override
  public String getConversionRateToIndianRupee() {
   return "82";
  }
 }

 private static final class DollarToRupee implements Currency {
  @Override
  public String getConversionRateToIndianRupee() {
   return "60";
  }
 }
 private static Currency createCurrencyFor(final String currencyStr) {
  if (currencyStr.equals(DOLLAR)) {
   return new DollarToRupee();
  }
```

```
    if (currencyStr.equals(EURO)) {
     return new EuroToRupee();
    }
    throw new IllegalArgumentException("Oops! no idea about <"
      + currencyStr + ">");
  }

  public static void main(String[] args) {
   System.out.println(createCurrencyFor(DOLLAR)
     .getConversionRateToIndianRupee());
   System.out.println(createCurrencyFor(EURO)
     .getConversionRateToIndianRupee());
   System.out.println(createCurrencyFor(YEN)
     .getConversionRateToIndianRupee());
  }
 }
```

All the knowledge of the conversion rule is in one place and hidden by design from the outside world. This hiding helps us edit existing rates and extend for more currencies all in one place. The big advantage is we get a single point where we can change, knowing the change will correctly reflect everywhere.

The Scala version

The Scala version is simpler, we just use the `apply` method:

```
trait Currency {
  def getConversionRateToIndianRupee: String
}


object CurrencyConverter {
  private object EuroToRupee extends Currency {
    override def getConversionRateToIndianRupee = "82"
  }

  private object DollarToRupee extends Currency {
    override def getConversionRateToIndianRupee = "60"
  }

  private object NoIdea extends Currency {
    override def getConversionRateToIndianRupee = "No Idea"
```

```
    }

    // the currency factory method
    // Note: Scala if statement is an expression.
    def apply(s: String):Currency = {
        if (s == "Dollar")  // same as s.equals("Dollar") in Java
DollarToRupee
        else if (s == "Euro")
          EuroToRupee
        else
          NoIdea
    }
}


val c = CurrencyConverter("Dollar") // apply method in action
c.getConversionRateToIndianRupee  // outputs "60"
```

Point to ponder: How could we rewrite the apply(...) method?

The apply method has one if expression, its value is the return value.

[Difference from Java. In Scala, the if/else statement has a value.]

This allows me to write:

```
scala> def m(x: Int) = if (x < 0) true else false
m: (x: Int)Boolean

scala> m(10)
res35: Boolean = false

scala> m(-10)
res36: Boolean = true
```

Builders

We need to model used cars for a resell shop. We want to rate a used car by kilometers driven, year of manufacture, make, model, accessories installed such as GPS, **Air Conditioning (AC)**, and safety features such as air bags and **anti-lock brakes (ABS)**. The list goes on and on.

Some of these attributes are mandatory and others are optional. For example, all cars will have the year of manufacture, kilometers driven, make and model. A car may not necessarily have GPS, AC, airbags or ABS.

We also need to validate the arguments. The kilometers are not negative, year of manufacture is something sensible (for example, not 1425 A.D.), and the make and model should match—make as Maruti and model as Corolla should be flagged as an error.

To handle all these requirements, we use the **Builder** pattern. Here is the UML diagram and then the code follows:

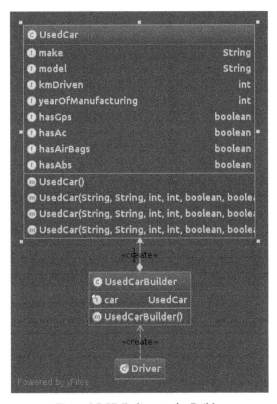

Figure 2.5: UML diagram for Builder

```
public class UsedCar {
  private String make;
  private String model;
  private int kmDriven;
  private int yearOfManufacturing;

  private boolean hasGps;
```

```java
  private boolean hasAc;
  private boolean hasAirBags;
  private boolean hasAbs;
        // Setters/Getters not shown
  }

public class UsedCarBuilder {

 private final UsedCar car;

 public UsedCarBuilder() {
  car = new UsedCar();
 }

 public UsedCarBuilder hasAirBags(final boolean b) {
  car.setHasAirBags(b);
  return this;
 }

 public UsedCarBuilder hasAbs(final boolean b) {
  car.setHasAbs(b);
  return this;
 }

 public UsedCarBuilder hasAc(final boolean b) {
  car.setHasAc(b);
  return this;
 }

 public UsedCarBuilder hasGps(final boolean b) {
  car.setHasGps(b);
  return this;
 }

 public UsedCarBuilder yearOfManufacturing(final int year) {
  car.setYearOfManufacturing(year);
  return this;
 }

 public UsedCarBuilder kmDriven(final int km) {
  car.setKmDriven(km);
```

```
    return this;
  }

  public UsedCarBuilder model(final String itsModel) {
   car.setModel(itsModel);
   return this;
  }

  public UsedCarBuilder make(final String itsMake) {
   car.setMake(itsMake);
   return this;
  }

  public UsedCar build() {
   // set sensible defaults for optional attributes - gps, ac, airbags,
abs
   // check make and model are consistent
   // check year of manufacturing is sensible
   // check kmDriven is not negative
   return car;
  }
}

public class Driver {
 public static void main(String[] args) {
  // Note the method chaining
  UsedCar car = new UsedCarBuilder().make("Maruti").model("Alto")
  .kmDriven(10000).yearOfManufacturing(2006).hasGps(false)
  .hasAc(false).hasAbs(false).hasAirBags(false).build();
  System.out.println(car);
 }
}
```

We design it like this for method chaining. Note the `build()` method of `UsedCarBuilder`. We get one place where we can check all the parameters rigorously before we return the `UsedCar object`. Making sure all fields satisfy the preconditions ensures the client code is not violating the contract.

Please see: `http://www.javaworld.com/article/2074956/learn-java/icontract--design-by-contract-in-java.html` for more information.

Ease of object creation

Let's say instead of using the builder pattern, could we use overloaded constructors?

Java allows us to overload constructors. And to promote reuse, we can always call other constructors using this (`arg1, arg2, ..., argN`) syntax:

```
public UsedCar(String make, String model, int kmDriven,
   int yearOfManufacturing, boolean hasGps, boolean hasAc,
   boolean hasAirBags, boolean hasAbs) {
super();
this.make = make;
this.model = model;
this.kmDriven = kmDriven;
this.yearOfManufacturing = yearOfManufacturing;
this.hasGps = hasGps;
this.hasAc = hasAc;
this.hasAirBags = hasAirBags;
this.hasAbs = hasAbs;
   }


 public UsedCar(String make, String model, int kmDriven,
    int yearOfManufacturing, boolean hasGps, boolean hasAc,
    boolean hasAirBags) {
  this(make, model, kmDriven, yearOfManufacturing, hasGps, hasAc,
hasAirBags, false); // no ABS
  }
 public UsedCar(String make, String model, int kmDriven,
    int yearOfManufacturing, boolean hasGps, boolean hasAc) {
  this(make, model, kmDriven, yearOfManufacturing, hasGps, hasAc,
false); // no Air Bags, no ABS
  }
```

The overloaded constructors keep getting narrower, tapering like a telescope. The fancy term for them is telescopic constructors:

Figure 2.6: Telescopic constructors

Anytime you want to create a `UserCar` object, you need to look up the list and use the right one. Now if you add some more optional parameters, the number of constructors blows up this is hard to maintain. If you wanted any combination of optional parameters, the number of constructors would exponentially increase.

One should be able to pick and choose any of the optional parameters in any order. The builder pattern makes this possible.

The other alternative is providing setters. Not that appealing as the onus is on the calling code to invoke the correct setters and to call the validate method to make sure the object state is as expected. Someone can forget calling the validate method.

On the other hand, the builder's method chaining style makes our code more readable and saves us from looking up the constructor args list by naming the arguments. It is a small language (almost) — helping us with complex object creation — called a **Domain Specific Language (DSL)**.

Scala shines again

It is pretty easy (again) in Scala. Made easy by Scala's support for named arguments and the wonderful case classes:

```
object Builder extends App {
  case class UsedCar(make: String, // 1
                     model: String,
                     kmDriven: Int,
                     yearOfManufacturing: Int,
                     hasGps: Boolean = false,
                     hasAc: Boolean = false,
                     hasAirBags: Boolean = false,
                     hasAbs: Boolean = false) {
    require(yearOfManufacturing > 1970, "Incorrect year") // 2
```

```
require(checkMakeAndModel(), "Incorrect make and model")

def checkMakeAndModel() = if (make == "Maruti") {
  model == "alto"
} else if (make == "Toyota") {
  model == "Corolla"
} else {
  true
}
}
  val usedMaruti = UsedCar(model = "alto", make = "Maruti", kmDriven =
10000, yearOfManufacturing = 1980, hasAbs = true, hasAirBags = true) // 3
  println(usedMaruti)
  val usedCorolla = usedMaruti.copy(make = "Toyota", model = "Corolla")
// 4
  println(usedCorolla)
  // val wrongModel = usedCorolla.copy(model = "alto") // throws -
Incorrect make and model
}
```

The salient points for the preceding code are as follows:

- The case class creates immutable fields of the same name.
- We check the preconditions with require — require is defined in `Predef` — and we use it to check the preconditions.
- Parameters can be named — so we don't need to look up the order. In fact, IDEs can autocomplete parameters for you — this is quite convenient.
- We can create another, almost identical, object with a few changes with the `copy` method.

The `Predef` is an object that provides many helpful goodies. It is imported automatically. `Predef` provides **implicit conversion,** which makes the following snippet work:

```
scala> "Hello World & Good Morning!".partition(x => x.isUpper ||
x.isLower)
res0: (String, String) = (HelloWorldGoodMorning," & !")
```

`Predef` also provides the `println` method we are using.

Summary

We looked at three creational design patterns—Singleton, Factory method, and builder— specifically the rationale behind them and the Java implementations. We also learnt about a special singleton—Null Object. We saw how Scala helps avoid null using Options. We looked at multiple Scala idioms with respect to Options and saw how Options as a container theme helps. We also saw the special apply method and learned how this syntactic sugar sweetens the code. Finally we looked at builders—a design pattern for creating objects with many attributes. We also saw how Scala's case classes help us with the creation of objects having many attributes. Take a deep breath readers, grab a cup of your favorite hot beverage and settle down to read about recursion.

3
Recursion and Chasing your Own Tail

In the first chapter, we wrote a nested method, `groupThem()`, that called itself. In the second chapter, the BST traversal method is similar to the nested method. We saw that the method calls itself to traverse the children. A method calling itself is **recursion**. In the previous chapter, we also touched upon tail recursion and Scala's `@tailrec` annotation.

Let's look at these concepts more closely and see how all these help us write succinct code, and how going recursive promotes immutability. In this chapter, we will first look at **recursive structures** — a structure is **recursive if the shape of the whole recurs** in the shape of the parts. We will then look at how Scala's pattern matching helps us to work on the composing parts. Next, we will take a look at a possible problem with very large structures and the mechanism to deal with them — namely **tail call optimization** (TCO) and `@tailrec` annotations. Finally, we will get a handle on **persistent data structures** and **structural sharing** to avoid needless copying while preserving immutability.

Recursive structures

The `find` command on Linux (and the `dir /s` command on Windows) recursively descends into a directory; if there are a few subdirectories within command, then it descends into each subdirectory, one by one. If the subdirectories, in turn, have subdirectories, command goes into each one and repeats the process all over again till all the directories are traversed. Let's have a look at the following directory:

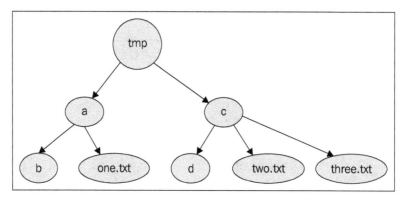

Figure 3.1: A directory tree is a recursive structure

Given this directory, try the following command:

```
% find ./tmp -type f -exec wc -c {} \;
```

The `find` command starts at the `tmp` directory and applies the `wc` command to each regular file (so for this example, skip directories).

The command enters in `tmp` and finds **a** and **c**. As these are directories, the flow enters **a** first, and finds **b** and `one.txt`. As directory **b** is empty, it looks at `one.txt` for which the predicate type `f` is true. So, the characters are counted for `one.txt`, and then the flow comes back to **a** and recurs into **c**. The process continues till every node in the directory tree is visited; also, every node is visited once and only once. Now, if you look carefully, when we come to node **a**, we have the same problem to solve as when we started with `tmp`. This problem is inherently recursive. This is the **essence of recursion**—we keep reducing the problem by dividing the dataset into smaller and smaller pieces. At some point though, we need to look at solving the problem (counting characters in regular files in our case). In our case, when we don't have any more directories to recur into, forms a base case with following cases:

- A subdirectory is empty—the flow just returns in this case.
- The note is not a directory at all but a regular file (`one.txt`). We perform the operation (count characters) and return.

The sub-problems that are solved directly without dividing it any further. Such base cases allow the algorithm to terminate eventually.

In the previous chapter, we looked at the binary tree traversal method. When the traversal flow hits the `Null` object, it terminates the traversal. This is a **base case**. Similarly, when the insertion flow hits the `Null` object, it adds the new node, forming another base case. When the traversal hits an intermediate node, we have a **recursive case**.

Pattern matching

Slice and dice is defined as the process of breaking something down (for example, information) into smaller parts to examine and understand it. You can get more information about slice and dice at:

`http://dictionary.reference.com/browse/slice-and-dice`

Let's see this technique in action. We will try to count the number of elements in `List`. There is already a length method defined on Lists:

```scala
scala> List(1,2,3).length
res0: Int = 3
```

Rolling out one of our own list teaches us something:

```scala
object Count extends App {
def count(list: List[Int]): Int = list match {
  case Nil => 0  // 1
  case head :: tail => 1 + count(tail) // 2
}
val l = List(1,2,3,4,5)
println(count(l)) // prints 5
  }
```

The preceding code counts the number of elements in the list. We match the list against two possible cases, which are as follows:

- **The base case**: The list is `Nil`, and an empty list matches `Nil` as it has zero elements, we return 0.

- **The general case**: This is a list that has one or more elements. A list with at least one element (**head**) plus possibly more elements (**tail**), we very well could have none. We don't know (as yet). So, we call the same method recursively with the **tail**. Here is the process shown pictorially:

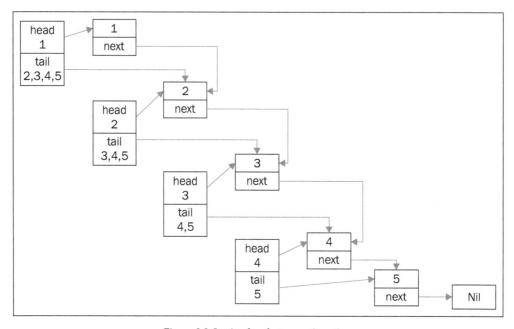

Figure 3.2: Losing head at every iteration

Note how we've left `head` aside in the preceding figure. We have taken the head value into account; in this case, we've incremented the count by 1. When we call the method recursively, we have one less element to process. This losing of the head and reducing finally land us with the case 1 — letting us terminate the processing eventually. We are **iterating** the list and **visiting** each node, albeit in a different way. Here, we don't use any mutation. There are no variables (no `var` keyword) used as loop counters. By avoiding loop counters (which would have to be var), recursion promotes immutability. Immutability is a boon when we write concurrent code, as we will soon see in the following chapters.

Deconstruction with case statements

Here is how we de-structure a list to get at the first element of the list. The following case clause splits the list into the first element (the head) and the rest of the list (the tail):

```
case head :: tail => 1 + count(tail)
```

These case matches when it is matched against a list with at least one element. Open the REPL and type the following code:

```scala
scala> val head :: tail = List(1, 2, 3, 4)  // 1
head: Int = 1
tail: List[Int] = List(2, 3, 4)
scala> val (x,y) = (7, 10)  // 2
x: Int = 7
y: Int = 10
```

The salient points for the preceding code are as follows:

- Deconstructs a list into its head, 1, and its tail, List(2, 3, 4).

- Deconstructs a pair into its constituent values—assigns 7 to x and 10 to y

And the case clause using underscore is as shown:

```scala
scala> List(1, 2, 3, 4) match {
     |    case head :: tail => println(head)  // 3
     |    case _ => println("Nothing")
     | }
```

 The case clause with just an underscore. We use it as an unnamed variable, just a placeholder.

The preceding command will print 1.

The :: symbol is a List extractor (refer to http://www.artima.com/pins1ed/extractors.html for more information on extractors). The x :: y expression results in a call to the unapply method of the :: object. You did read it right. The :: symbol is a case class and its companion object is: :. Like the apply method that we saw earlier, the Scala compiler will call unapply in a pattern matching expression. When we define a case class, we get both the apply and unapply methods written for us:

```scala
scala> case class MyClass (x: Int, y: Int)
defined class MyClass

scala> val p = MyClass(1, 2);
p: MyClass = MyClass(1,2)

scala> p match {
```

```
    |    case MyClass(a, b) => println(s"a=$a, b=$b")    // 1
    | }
a=1, b=2


scala> p match {
    |    case a MyClass b => println(s"a=$a, b=$b")    // 2
    | }
a=1, b=2
```

At the part in the code labeled as 2, the extractor expression is written in the infix form:

```
scala> val p = List(1, 2, 3, 4)
p: List[Int] = List(1, 2, 3, 4)


scala>  p match {
    |       case ::(head, tail) => println(s"head=$head, tail=$tail") // 1
    |       case _ => println("What's up???")
    |    }
head=1, tail=List(2, 3, 4)
```

The part of code labeled as 1, the unapply method of : : is called. The statement is just rewritten in an infix notation as follows:

```
        case head :: tail => println(s"head=$head, tail=$tail")
```

Stack overflows

Our recursive solution works, however there is a problem waiting to strike us. The code works fine for small lists with a few elements. Let's stress test it with a big list that has 20000 elements:

1. Call the count method as shown in the following code:

   ```
   val l  = 1 to 20000 // A range object
   count(l.toList) // Converts the range into a list
   ```

2. Run the code, and you will get the java.lang.StackOverflowError error. The problem here is the recursive call 1 + count (tail).

Each intermediate context is remembered on a stack frame. The intermediate context here is **Get me a count of the tail, and add one to it**. How many such intermediate contexts are there? I think you already guessed it right, they are equal to the number of elements in a list.

In other words, the numbers of contexts to remember are proportional to n. In algorithmic sense, these are equal to O(n). So for this example list, we need 20,000 stack frames for a list that has 20,000 elements; so, we need these many stack frames. The system usually cannot allocate these many. Hence, the routine looks broken.

Now, what good is the technique if it does not work for large lists? We are in a logjam, as you can see in the following figure:

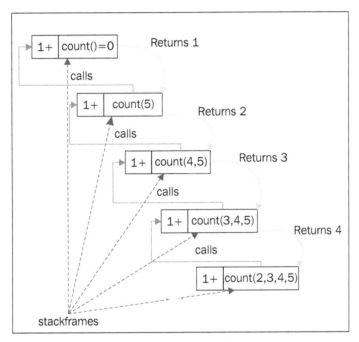

Figure 3.3: An example of stack overflow

Tail recursion to the rescue

There is a technique, an optimization really, that helps us get out of the logjam. However, we need to tweak the code a bit for this. We will make the recursive call as the last and only call. This means that there is no intermediate context to remember. This last and only call is called the **tail call**. Code in this tail call form is amenable to TCO. Scala generates code that, behind the scenes, uses a loop — the generated code does not use any stack frames:

```scala
import scala.annotation.tailrec


def count(list: List[Int]): Int = {
  @tailrec    // 1
  def countIt(l: List[Int], acc: Int): Int = l match {
    case Nil => acc // 2
    case head :: tail => countIt(tail, acc+1)  // 3
  }
  countIt(list, 0)
}
```

The changes are like this:

We have a nested workhorse method that is doing all the hard work. The `count` method calls the `countIt` nested recursive method, with the list it got in the argument, and an accumulator. The earlier intermediate context is now expressed as an accumulator expression with the help of the following steps:

1. The `@tailrec` annotation makes sure that we are doing the right things so that we benefit from the TCO. Without `@tailrec`, Scala may apply the optimization or it may not. The `@tailrec` annotation is a helping hand to ensure that the function call is optimized. Try the same annotation on our first version. You will get a compilation error.

2. Play time: Change the second case in the previous code as shown:
    ```scala
    case head :: tail => {

      val cnt: Int = countIt(tail, acc + 1)

        println(cnt)

        cnt

    }
    ```

3. You will get a compilation error after changing the second case:

   ```
   Error: could not optimize @tailrec annotated method countIt: it
   contains a recursive call not in tail position
   ```

4. When the execution lands in this clause, we are at the end of the list. We are not going to find any more elements, so the base case just returns the accumulator.

5. There is no intermediate context now – just a tail call. This is the only and last recursive call. We found one more element. We increment the accumulator to record the fact and pass it on.

Compared to the earlier version, why does this version work? If the compiler can use tail call optimization, then it does not need to stack up the context. So, no stack frames are needed as the resulting executable code uses loops behind the scenes.

Getting the nth element of a list

A list holds a certain number of elements. The first element is at index 0, and the second element at index 1. If the index is out of range, we get an exception.

We will write a method to find the nth element of a list. This method will return an option. If n is out of bounds, we will return None. Otherwise, we will return Some(elem). Let's look at the code and then a diagram to understand it better:

```scala
import scala.annotation.tailrec
object NthElemOfList extends App {
  def nth(list: List[Int], n: Int): Option[Int] = {
   @tailrec
   def nthElem(list: List[Int], acc: (Int, Int)): Option[Int] = list
match {
     case Nil => None
     case head :: tail => {
       if (acc._1 == acc._2)      // 1
       Some(head)
       else
         nthElem(tail, (acc._1 + 1, acc._2))      // 2
     }
    }
   nthElem(list, (0, n))    // 3
  }
  val bigList = 1 to 100000 toList   // 4
  println(nth(List(1, 2, 3, 4, 5, 6), 3).getOrElse("No such elem"))
  println(nth(List(1, 2, 3, 4, 5, 6), 300).getOrElse("No such elem"))
  println(nth(bigList, 2333).getOrElse("No such elem"))
}
```

Here is a diagrammatic representation of the flow:

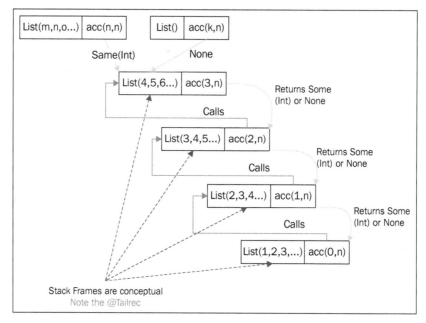

Figure: 3.4: Conceptual stack frames

The description of the preceding diagram is as follows:

- Our accumulator is a pair. The first element is a running index and holds the index of the current node, starting from **0**. The second element is always fixed at **n**.

- If index == n, we have found the element. Now, we will return it wrapped in a some. else we increase the running index and recursively call the method again on the tail of the list.

- We wish to hide the accumulator from the client code. Keeping an accumulator is an implementation detail.

- We will test the index with a very big list as @tailrec is in effect, the TCO kicks in and we don't get any stack overflows. Try to rewrite the preceding code without using a pair of element for the accumulator. Compare your version with it and check which one is better.

The following are a few points that we need to ponder:

- Could we simply use acc as Int? Do we really need the pair?

- Try writing the code so that we decrement the accumulator instead of incrementing it.

An expression parser

We will look at an instructive example of how recursion and immutability go hand in hand. We will look at an infix expression parser.

 An infix notation is where the operator comes in between two operands, for example, 3+4+5-6 is the infix notation.

We will look at the iterative Java version and then at the recursive Scala version. We support only operators + and * and also provide bracketed sub-expressions.

Evaluating *(1+2)*3*(2+4)* expression should give us the output as *54* and evaluating *(1+2)*3+4* expression should give us the output as *13*. The grammar for our expression parser looks as shown in the following code. Note how each sub-expression is an expression composed of other sub-expressions, terms, and factors. In short, the grammar is recursively defined. Here is the grammar:

```
Expr: Term | Term + Expr
Term: Factor | Factor * Term
Factor: [0-9][0-9]+ | '(' Expr ')'
```

Here is a diagrammatic representation of the flow:

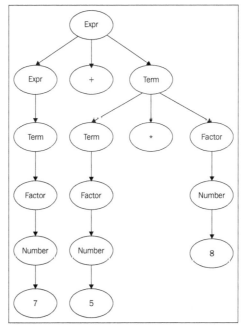

Figure 3.5: The expression tree

Look at the bracketed expression node in the bottom-right corner of the preceding image. The grammar also tells us that multiplication (*) is given precedence over addition (+). A bracketed expression has the highest precedence. Here is the Java code which makes use of an `tokenizer`:

```java
import java.util.regex.Matcher;
import java.util.regex.Pattern;

import org.apache.commons.lang3.Validate;

public class Parser {

 private static final String L_BRACKET = "(";
 private static final String R_BRACKET = ")";

 private class Tokenizer {

  private static final String NUM_PATTERN = "(\\d+).*";
  private String s;
  private final Pattern p;

  public Tokenizer(final String s) {
   this.s = s;
   this.p = Pattern.compile(NUM_PATTERN);
  }

  public boolean nextTokenIs(final String tok) {
   if (s.isEmpty()) {
    return false;
   }
   return s.startsWith(tok);
  }

  public void consume(final String tok) {
   s = s.replaceFirst(Pattern.quote(tok), "");
  }

  public boolean nextTokenIsNumber() {
   return s.matches(NUM_PATTERN);
  }

  public int consumeANumber() {
   if (s.matches(NUM_PATTERN)) {
    final Matcher m = p.matcher(s);
```

```
      Validate.isTrue(m.matches(), "Could not extract number
from <"+ s + ">");
      final String numStr = m.group(1);
      s = s.replaceFirst(Pattern.quote(numStr), "");
      return Integer.valueOf(numStr);
    }

    throw new IllegalArgumentException("Number expected");
  }

};

private final Tokenizer tokenizer;

public Parser(final String s) {
 tokenizer = new Tokenizer(s);
}

private int factor() {
 if (tokenizer.nextTokenIsNumber()) {
  final int num = tokenizer.consumeANumber(); // 1
  return num;
 }
 if (tokenizer.nextTokenIs(L_BRACKET)) {
  tokenizer.consume(L_BRACKET); // 2
  final int num = expr();
  if (!tokenizer.nextTokenIs(R_BRACKET)) {
   throw new IllegalArgumentException("Syntax error - ) missing");
  }
  tokenizer.consume(R_BRACKET);   // 3
  return num;
 }
 throw new IllegalArgumentException("Either number or (expected");
}

private int term() {
 int val = factor();      // 4
 while (tokenizer.nextTokenIs("*")) { // 5
  tokenizer.consume("*");
  val *= factor(); //  6
 }
 return val;
}

public int expr() {
```

```
    int val = term();              //  7
    while (tokenizer.nextTokenIs("+")) {    // 8
     tokenizer.consume("+");
     val += term();    // 9
    }
    return val;
   }
 }
```

We have a very simple `tokenizer` class; it splits an input string into tokens, for example, given the expression *(111+222)*, it generates *(, 111, +, 222,)*. Although it is a pretty simple `tokenizer`, it is sufficient for our needs. We use Java's regular expression matching facilities to tokenize our string with the help of the following steps:

1. The code obeys the preceding grammar. A factor is either a number or a subexpression starting with ' ('.

2. If it is a number, we consume and return it. If it is a sub-expression instead, we process the sub-expression first. So given the expression *(9+4)*4*, we first evaluate *9+4*.

3. Once we have reduced the subexpression into a number, we consume ') ', thereby consuming all the bracketed subexpressions, and return the number to the caller.

4. After the bracketed subexpression, multiplication has a higher precedence. However, any term (multiplication) starts with a factor.

5. Once we have consumed a factor, if the next token is a *, we consume it too.

6. We keep looking for more terms. Once all the terms are reduced to a number, we return the resulting number.

7. This is the topmost method. It tries to reduce to a term. Term could be a simple number though.

8. While we have + next in the stream, we keep looking for more addition expressions.

9. We keep adding the reduced values to get the value of the overall expression.

Try the input `(1+2))`. How would you fix it?

Try rewriting the code using recursion. What could we say about TCO the Java Virtual Machine?

Here is the code for the Scala version:

```scala
import scala.annotation.tailrec

object Parser extends App {

  val Number = """^(\d+).*""".r        // 1
  val LParen = """^[(].*""".r

  def factor(f: String): (String, Int) = f match {
    case Number(d) => (f.drop(d.length), d.toInt) // 2
    case LParen(_*) => {
      val p = expr(f.drop(1), 0)   // 3
      val e = p._1
      if (e.take(1) == ")") {   // 4
        (e.drop(1), p._2)
      } else {
        throw new IllegalArgumentException("Right bracket missing")
      }
    }
    case _ => throw new IllegalArgumentException("Number or sub-
expression expected")
  }

  @tailrec
  def term(t: String, acc: Int): (String, Int) = {
    val p = factor(t)
    val e = p._1

    if (e.take(1) == "*") {                    // 5
      term(e.drop(1), acc * p._2)        // 6
    } else {
      (e, acc * p._2)                          // 7
    }
  }

  @tailrec
  def expr(s: String, acc: Int): (String, Int) = {
    val p = term(s, 1)
    val e = p._1

    if (e.take(1) == "+") {                    // 8
      expr(e.drop(1), acc + p._2)        // 9
    } else {
```

```
        (e, acc + p._2)                                    // 10
    }
}

def expr(s: String): Int = {
  val e = expr(s, 0)
  e._2
}

val p = expr("(1+2)*3*(2+4)")
println(p)
}
```

Since the execution flow is a bit involved, the following diagram will help you understand it:

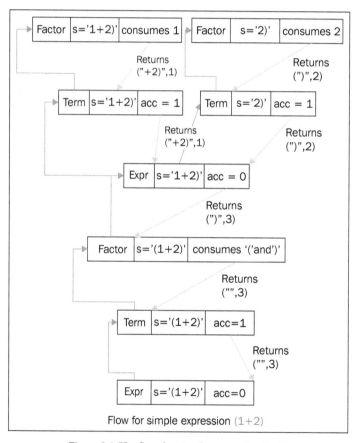

Flow for simple expression (1+2)

Figure 3.6: The flow for simple expression (1+2)

We will create a regular expression pattern—Regex—to match a number. We use a multiline string, so we don't need to escape the backslash character. To match digits, we simply use \d instead of \\d.

To match and extract either a number or ' (', we use Regex as an extractor in a pattern match:

```scala
scala> val num = """(\d+)([.]\d+)?""".r
num: scala.util.matching.Regex = (\d+)([.]\d+)?


scala> "101.22" match {
     |    case num(decimal, fractional) => s"decimal = $decimal,
fractional = $fractional"
     | }
res0: String = decimal = 101, fractional = .22
```

The salient points for the preceding code are as follows:

- This is a call to evaluate a sub-expression that is enclosed in brackets. For 2*(3+3), the 3+3 addition precedes multiplication.
- The closing ') ' bracket is consumed. This indicates the completed evaluation of a bracketed sub-expression.
- We are in the middle of a term.
- A term keeps evaluating itself and other subsequent terms. Refer to the grammar diagram.
- Now, we that are done evaluating a term, we can return the remaining string and the result of the term evaluation.
- We are in the middle of an expression.
- Keep evaluating—giving precedence to a term evaluation.
- Finally, return the pair of the leftover string and the result of the overall expression.

Take a somewhat bigger expression and work through the code.

When we mix string and regular expressions, we often see the leaning toothpick syndrome. The regular expression notation, \d, matches a digit character. However, the backslash also works as an escape character. You need to double the backslash so that the Regex engine can see it, for example:

```
scala> val regex = "H\\dllo".r
regex: scala.util.matching.Regex = H\dllo
scala> regex findFirstIn("H1llo H2llo")
res0: Option[String] = Some(H1llo)
```

Scala's triple quote strings allow us to express the regular expression in a natural way. Now, try using the following expression in the preceding code snippet:

```
val regex = """H\dllo""".r
```

Persistent data structures

As you can guess by now, immutability is the underlying big theme. The following Java code reverses a list in place:

```
List<Integer> list = Lists.newArrayList(1,2,3,4);
// List<Integer> refList = Lists.newArrayList(list); // 1
List<Integer> refList = list;
Collections.reverse(list);

System.out.println(list);
System.out.println(refList);
```

The problem is when we do the reversal in place, the code using the list as a reference also sees the change. To prevent this, we need to use the statement at the part labeled as 1—the defensive copy technique. The other problem with changing the list in place is thread safety. We need to carefully synchronize the list access so we stay away from heisenbugs. To know more about them, refer to

http://opensourceforu.efytimes.com/2010/10/joy-of-programming-types-of-bugs/

Scala, instead, advocates immutable lists; we cannot change the list structure in place; instead, we create a new list:

```scala
import scala.annotation.tailrec

object ReverseAList extends App {

@tailrec
def reverseList(list: List[Int], acc: List[Int]) : List[Int] = list match
{
  case head :: tail => reverseList(tail, head :: acc)
  case Nil => acc
}
val l = 1 to 20000 toList

println(reverseList(l, Nil))
}
```

We will again use the **accumulator idiom** to make the list tail recursive. As Scala's `List` is immutable, we need to create a new list each time a new node is added. You may ask, won't it be expensive to create a brand new list each time? Not really, as the lists are immutable and they could be structurally shared as shown in the following figure:

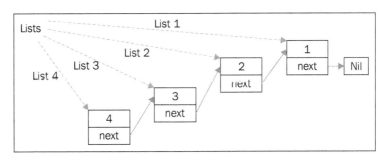

Figure 3.7: An example of lists

As shown pictorially in the preceding diagram, we can traverse **list 2**. As the node (value 3) is added, both **list 3** and **list 2** can share the node with the value **1** and the node with value **2**. As both these lists are immutable, the nodes could be safely shared.

Such a data structure that always preserves the previous version of itself when it is modified is a persistent data structure. And no, it has nothing to do with persistence as in disk/database persistence.

Let's look at the following list concatenation:

```
val l1 = List(1,2,3)
val l2 = List(4,5,6)
val l3 = l1 ++ l2   // List(1,2,3,4,5,6)
```

Here, we need to copy `l1` nodes and structurally share `l2` nodes.

 We cannot just change `l1` as it is immutable. We need to copy `l1` nodes to `l3` and change the third node to point at `l2` so that anyone who is already referring to `l1` is not affected.

Now, let's try our hand at an example. In following diagram, link up the left-hand side dangling pointer of the node with value **4** so that the tree is structurally shared. Draw the shared structure after inserting 22 in the tree:

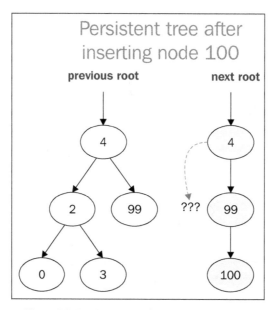

Figure 3.8: Persistent tree after inserting node 100

Two forms of recursion

In the previous sections, we saw the tail recursive code to reverse a list. Take a look at this form:

```scala
object ReverseAList1 extends App {
 def reverseList(list: List[Int]): List[Int] = list match {
 case head :: tail => reverseList(tail) :+ head
 case Nil => Nil
 }
 val l = (1 to 20000).toList
 println(reverseList(l))
}
```

I know. This form is not tail recursive. Hence, this form will not benefit from the tail call optimization. Try to put the @tailrec annotation on the reverseList method. You will get a compilation error.

This form is still useful though. There are times when we do not want all the list elements. We just want to look at the first few elements of the result. We want to make the recursive call evaluation deferred. Call is not computed upfront. Instead, it is only evaluated when needed. We are talking of delayed evaluation in this case. Scala's **Streams** implements lazy lists where elements are only evaluated when they are needed. We will look in detail at the lazy evaluation in the upcoming chapter and how solutions that are not tail recursive would be better candidates to build streams.

Summary

You learned about recursion and problems that are by nature, recursive. For example, directories on a Linux filesystem are defined this way. You also learned about recursive solutions, the general case, and the essential base case. The base case is needed so that the process eventually gets terminates. We also looked at Scala's slice and dice technique and how to split the list so that we can visit each element. We saw how recursive calls and associated context are remembered on stack frames and the need for tail recursion. We saw examples where tail recursion enables TCO. We looked at a detail example of a small expression parser. We looked at how recursive code promotes immutability, as we did not use var in our code. We looked at persistent data structures and the two forms of recursion. Let's now move on to the wonders of Scala's power features for delayed evaluation.

4
Lazy Sequences – Being Lazy, Being Good

In life, we (hopefully) spend money only on things that we really need. For example, I keep eyeing those ever powerful laptops being advertised every day. I drool over those shiny machines with hefty RAM sizes and lightening processor speed. The **buy** button is so inviting!

I am sure, at times, you must have felt similar buying urges. However, as you know well, we just don't buy it willy nilly. We think, plan, and buy if we really need it. Simply, because we have limited money, we need to spend it carefully.

A software system, too, has limited resources. When a system needs to acquire an expensive resource, the resource should be obtained when it is really needed, that is at its first use. If the system goes and acquire all expensive resources up front, a reducing lot of overhead would be incurred. Deferring resource acquisition, till it is needed, is an important design principle. For example, a while ago, we looked at singletons. Singletons make sure that objects exist uniquely while the program is running. Singletons are also used to lazy initialize the object they wrap. In case the object is never needed, it is never initialized.

So, whenever we don't create objects upfront, but strictly **on demand**, are examples of a generic pattern, **Lazy Acquisition**. We acquire something when we really need it.

Lazy evaluation is a special case of Lazy Acquisition. We will look at lazy evaluation in this chapter. Laziness is very useful when we compute only on demand. We may not need all of the result—so why perform the expensive computation in advance? We will look at the proxy design pattern used to implement laziness. We will also see how a highly popular **Object Relational Mapping (ORM)** library, Hibernate, uses proxies to lazy load entity objects. Next, you will learn about Scala's lazy keyword. We will use our friend, the REPL, and play a bit with some examples first. It will give us some practice of lazy evaluation. We will see a related theme, memoization. Scala's by name evaluation comes next. Expressing parameters by name is yet one more form of lazy evaluation. Finally, we will look at Scala Streams. Streams are lazy lists, an implementation of infinite sequences. Traversing an infinite sequences just keeps going forever, it never terminates.

Illusion and reality – the proxy pattern

Many of us have come across the term **proxy server**. At a large company, the Internet access is restricted by a proxy server. The company may provide access to work-related pages only. Social media sites may be blocked. The proxy server is the place where all these rules are built. It is a checkpoint. A proxy is a class, hiding the real thing. It essentially is an interface (not to confuse with Java interface) to an expensive object. The real object could possibly be a remote object.

The proxy pattern is used to implement cross-cutting concerns. A cross-cutting concern is:

- A functionality needed across many different modules of an application
- The functionality is not core to the application (it would be reused by another application too)
- The functionality is necessary in most application (you need it very much—at times simply cannot do without it)

You don't want to reinvent the wheel and reimplement the functionality every time. Security, for example, is a cross-cutting concern. Transaction management is another example. Caching is another cross-cutting concern.

The Spring framework uses the proxy pattern extensively to realize security and transaction management. Refer to `https://springframework.guru/proxy-pattern/` for more information.

The following is the UML diagram:

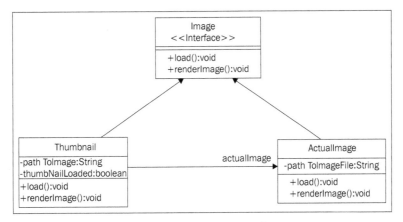

Figure 4.1: Proxy pattern - UML diagram

The code is as follows for the proxy pattern:

```
public interface Image {
 public void load();
 public void renderImage();
}

public class ActualImage implements Image { // 1
 private final String pathToImageFile;

 public ActualImage(final String pathToImageFile) {
  super();
  this.pathToImageFile = pathToImageFile;
 }
 @Override
 public void renderImage() {
  System.out.println("Rendering image <" + pathToImageFile + ">");
 }
 @Override
 public void load() {
  System.out.println("Loading image from file <" + pathToImageFile +
">");
 }
}

public class Thumbnail implements Image { // 2

 private final String pathToImage;
```

```
  private final ActualImage actualImage;
  private boolean thumbNailLoaded;

  public Thumbnail(final String pathToImage) { // 3
    super();
    this.pathToImage = pathToImage;
    this.thumbNailLoaded = false;
    this.actualImage = new ActualImage(pathToImage);
  }

  @Override
  public void renderImage() {
    if (!thumbNailLoaded) { // 4
      load();
      thumbNailLoaded = true;
      System.out.println("Render the thumb nail");
    } else {
      actualImage.load();   // 5
      actualImage.renderImage();
    }
  }

  @Override
  public void load() {
    System.out.println("Loading Thumb Nail <" + pathToImage + ">");
  }
}
```

The salient points for the preceding code are as follows:

- This class holds the actual image. This image would take a lot of time to get loaded into memory. We want to load it on demand.
- The proxy class, proxy to the actual image.
- We cache the path to the actual image.
- First time, we load the thumbnail image.

- The next time someone asks us to render it again (maybe by clicking it again), we load the actual image and render it. Refer to the following figure:

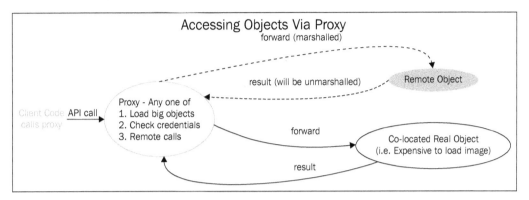

Figure 4.2: Proxy — execution flow

Hibernate's lazy loading

Hibernate exposes persistence-related database access via an object API. A Java class is mapped to a database table. A parent having many children is mapped as shown in the following code:

```
@Entity
public class Parent {

...

@OneToMany(mappedBy = "parent")
private Set<Child> children;

...

}
@Entity
public class Child {

...

@ManyToOne
@JoinColumn(name = "parent_id")
private Parent parent;

...

}
```

This maps the following table structure:

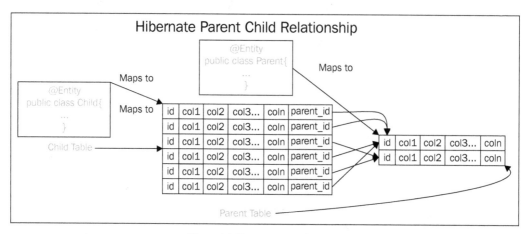

Figure 4.3: Proxying in Hibernate

The children are, by default, **lazy loaded**. This holds true for any mapped members that are collections. You may not need them all the time you load the parent. If you do, you can load them as needed. The set is actually a PersistenceSet, a proxy. The catch is that this is not completely transparent though. You need to have a hibernate session active to load the children. Otherwise, you get a `LazyInitializationException`.

Why is this done? The children may have children of their own. The object graph, parent → children → grand-children and so on, could be very large. So, it is loaded **as needed** and not upfront. Proxies to the rescue!!

 You can see more about a very popular library, CGLIB, for more on proxying at `http://jnb.ociweb.com/jnb/jnbNov2005.html`.

Lazy val – calling by need

Enough wandering in the Java wonderland! Coming back to Scala, we have vals and **lazy vals**. If some object creation is expensive, we can stick the **lazy** keyword before val to initialize it **on its first use**.

Open the REPL and try out the following:

```
scala> lazy val p = {
     |    println ("Initializing")
     |    9
     | }
p: Int = <lazy>
scala> println(p)
Initializing  // p accessed for the first time
9
scala> println(p) // cached result of p
9
```

We stick the `lazy` keyword before the `val` keyword. We are using a block expression to initialize p. In Scala, a block is a sequence of expressions enclosed in { }. The last expression in the block is the **value of the block**. The value of the block here is 9. On the other hand, the value of an assignment expression is Unit. The Unit type is equivalent to the `void` type in Java.

Infinite sequences – Scala streams

We have seen many examples of Scala's list. Lists are sequences. Moreover, lists are **strict** sequences. Meaning all elements of the list are constructed upfront. However, there are **non-strict** sequences, whose elements are constructed as needed.

A list is formed by connecting cons cells. There are two cases:

1. `1 :: Nil`

   In this case, the cons cell has a value and the empty list as a tail. This list has only one element. Let's fire up the REPL and try the following snippets:

   ```
   scala> 1 :: Nil
   res2: List[Int] = List(1)
   ```

2. `1 :: 2 :: Nil`

   Here, we have the cons cell having a value and another list as a tail:

   ```
   scala> (1 :: (2 :: Nil)).tail
   res11: List[Int] = List(2)
   ```

A list with three elements looks like the following:

```
scala> val p = 4 :: 5 :: 6 :: Nil
p: List[Int] = List(4, 5, 6)
```

This version, could be rewritten as:

```
scala> val p = (4 :: (5 :: (6 :: Nil)))
p: List[Int] = List(4, 5, 6)
```

This version, in turn, could be written as:

```
scala> val p = ( ( (Nil.::(6)).::(5) ).::(4) )
val p = ( ( (Nil.::(6)).::(5) ).::(4) )
p: List[Int] = List(4, 5, 6)
```

The :: symbol is the cons (construct) operator. The second expression shows the way the cons operator binds. Nil is a list and we invoke the cons operator and grow the list.

Similarly, the operator + is used to append to a list:

```
scala> val list = List(1, 2, 3)
list: List[Int] = List(1, 2, 3)

scala> list :+ 4
res12: List[Int] = List(1, 2, 3, 4)
```

This appending needs to traverse all of the list to reach the last element and attach the new value. In other words, appending to a list has $O(n)$ complexity.

On the other hand, prepending using :: is $O(1)$. We don't need to traverse all of the list, as the head is readily available.

Hence, appending to the list is a costly operation as it takes time traversing the list for every appending operation.

Now, look at the following:

```
scala> var k = 2
k: Int = 2
scala> def f() = { k += 1; k }
f: ()Int
scala> lazy val p = Stream.continually( f() ) // 1
p: scala.collection.immutable.Stream[Int] = <lazy>
```

```
scala> (p take 4) foreach {x => println(x)} // 2
3
4
5
6
scala> p
res27: scala.collection.immutable.Stream[Int] = Stream(3, 4, 5, ?)
```

The method f gets converted to a function. The Stream.continually() method creates an infinite stream. It takes an a function. When we access each element, the function is called to compute that element.

As shown, the function is only called when the value is accessed. This on-demand executed function is also knows as a **Thunk**. Once the value is computed, it is cached for further access. This caching goes by the fancy name, memoization.

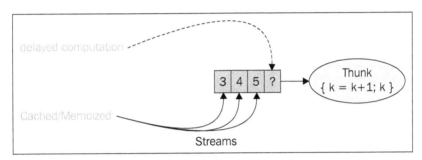

Figure 4.4: Thunks and Memoization

Recursive streams

We looked at recursion earlier. Recursive forms are defined in terms of themselves. For example, folders can have subfolders, which, in turn, can have subfolders themselves. Another example is recursive methods calling themselves.

We can use a similar form to define **recursive streams**. To define recursive streams, consider the following case:

```
scala> lazy val r = Stream.cons(1, Stream.cons(2, Stream.empty))
r: Stream.Cons[Int] = <lazy>
scala> (r take 4) foreach {x => println(x)}
1
2
```

How is this useful? The second cons call can be recursive. (Note we don't need any var):

```scala
scala> def s(n: Int):Stream[Int]  =
     |     Stream.cons(n, s(n+1))    // 1
s: (n: Int)Stream[Int]
scala> lazy val q = s(0)
q: Stream[Int] = <lazy>
```

Here, we construct the lazy list by placing a recursive call to the method, s.

However, the following form is a succinct one:

```scala
scala> def succ(n: Int):Stream[Int] = n #:: succ(n+1)
succ: (n: Int)Stream[Int]
scala> lazy val r = succ(1)
r: Stream[Int] = <lazy>
```

> Method parameters are val in Scala. Try the following REPL snippet:
> ```scala
> scala> def m(s: Int) =  s = s + 1
> <console>:8: error: reassignment to val
>        def m(s: Int) =  s = s + 1
> ```
> Why? Allowing assignment to input parameters is often seen as bad style and makes it harder to reason about code. If really required, you can assign the argument to var.
>
> Refer to https://sourcemaking.com/refactoring/remove-assignments-to-parameters for more on this code smell.
>
> In case you want to use vars, you need a temporary variable:
> ```scala
> scala> def m(s: Int) = {
>      |     var n = s + 1
>      |     n = n * 2
>      |     n
>      | }
> m: (s: Int)Int
> ```

Memoization and the flyweight pattern

Memoization is caching of oft-repeated computation results. This is a way to avoid recalculating the result again. **Flyweight** is a design pattern that uses memoization. A flyweight is an object that minimizes memory use by sharing. A very good example of a flyweight is Java's `Integer.valueOf(int)` method.

Java supports **autoboxing** of primitives to corresponding wrapper types. We should always prefer. Let's have a look at the following snippet:

```
int someInt = ...;
Integer someInteger = someInt;
```

instead of the following:

```
new Integer(someInt);
```

If we happen to auto-box (int → Integer) values in the range of 128 to 127, the `valueOf()` method allows us to reuse the `Integer` object. As integer instances are immutable, we can rest easy about sharing the same integer instance across the application.

The following JUnit test case shows the memoization:

```
@Test
public void test() {
  Integer a1 = Integer.valueOf(12);
  Integer a2 = Integer.valueOf(12);

  Integer a3 = Integer.valueOf(12112);
  Integer a4 = Integer.valueOf(12112);

  assertSame(a1, a2); // a1 & a2 are the same object
  assertNotSame(a3, a4); // a3 & a4 need not be...

    }
```

Refer to the following figure that shows the integer memoization:

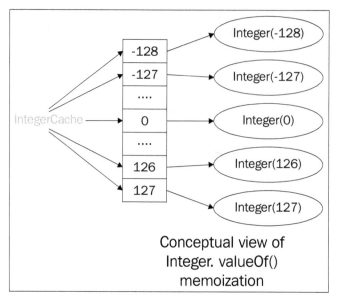

Figure 4.5: Integer memoization

Crossing over to the Scala wonderland, a Stream caches results, to avoid re-computation. The following is an REPL interaction:

```
scala> def f() = {
     |     println("previous value = " + k)
     |     k += 1;
     |     k
     | }
f: ()Int
scala> val p = Stream.continually( f() ) // 1
previous value = 3
p: scala.collection.immutable.Stream[Int] = Stream(4, ?)
scala> (p take 3) foreach { x => println(x) } // 2
4
previous value = 4
5
previous value = 5
6
scala> (p take 3) foreach { x => println(x) } // 3
```

4

5

6

We get the following findings when we dissect the code:

1. The `continually` method of Stream creates an infinite stream. The expression is a passed as an argument and is computed for each occurrence. In simpler words, each element of the lazy list is produced by calling the `f()` function. The `continually` method takes a by name parameter. We will soon see what are by name parameters.

2. When a new element is accessed, by the name argument, our function is called. We see the message printed from the function.

3. When the element is already computed, the stream cached the value. The function is not called as it is already computed and cached. So, we don't see the message anymore to avoid repetition.

Call by name

Typically, parameters are passed by value are by-value that is the value of the parameter is determined before it gets passed to the function. In the REPL session here, we have two functions, g and f.

We pass the value of calling `getValue()` to f and g:

```scala
scala> var k = 0
k: Int = 0
scala> def getVal() = {
     |     k += 1
     |     k
     | }
getVal: ()Int
scala> def g(i: Int) = {
     |     println(s"${i}")
     |     println(s"${i}")
     |     println(s"${i}")
     | }
```

```
g:  (i:  Int) Unit
```

```
scala> g(getVal())
1
1
1
```

Refer to the following figure:

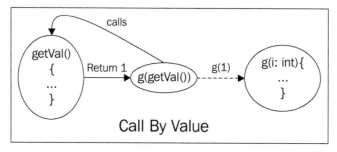

Figure 4.6: Call By Value

The three `println` statements in `g()` print the same value, `1`:

```
scala> def f(i: => Int) = {
     |    println(s"${i}")
     |    println(s"${i}")
     |    println(s"${i}")
     | }
f:  (i:  => Int) Unit
```

```
scala> k = 0
k: Int = 0
```

```
scala> f(getVal())
1
2
3
```

Refer to the following figure:

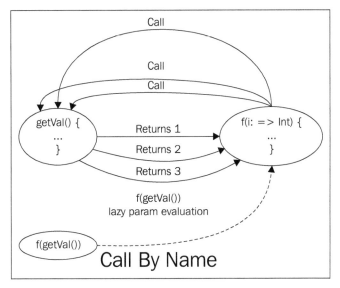

Figure 4.7: Call by name

The parameter, i, is evaluated **every time you ask for the value**. This is different from the lazy val. Lazy vals are computed for the first time and then the value is **cached**. If we don't refer to the parameter, it is never evaluated. The following is a code snippet illustrating the point:

```scala
scala> def g(i: Int) = {
     |    println("Not fine")
     | }
g: (i: Int)Unit
scala> def f(i: => Int) = {
     |    println("Am fine")
     | }
f: (i: => Int)Unit
scala> f(1/0)
Am fine
scala> g(1/0)
java.lang.ArithmeticException: / by zero
  ... 33 elided
```

We can get away with the illegal division by zero as long as we don't refer to the parameter! Not so with the g() call, as the parameter is evaluated by a value. The parameter value is evaluated beforehand, and the attempt to divide by the 0 results in an exception.

Let's consider the following definition of f:

```scala
scala> def f(i: => Int) = {
     |     lazy val k = i
     |     println(s"${k}")
     |     println(s"${k}")
     |     println(s"${k}")
     | }
f: (i: => Int)Unit

scala> var k = 0
k: Int = 0
scala> def getVal() = {
     |     // println("Yup!!!")
     |     k += 1
     |     k
     | }
getVal: ()Int
scala> f(getVal())
1
1
1
```

This is a common idiom. We get back the call of by value semantics by storing the call by name parameter into a local lazy val. The variable k is only evaluated when needed, and the value cached for subsequent use.

Uncomment the `println` line in `getVal()` and check the output. The message "Yup!!!" should be printed only once, the first time k (and hence i) is evaluated.

Streams are collections

Scala collections shine as we almost never need to explicitly loop over them. Using functional combinators like map, flatMap, and filter we get things done declaratively. This comes very handy, as we will soon see.

Streams are lazy lists. You guessed right—these are collections all right:

```
scala> def succ(n: Int):Stream[Int] = n #:: succ(n+1)
succ: (n: Int)Stream[Int]


scala> lazy val r = succ(0)
r: Stream[Int] = <lazy>
scala> println(r.take(10).mkString(" + "))
0 + 1 + 2 + 3 + 4 + 5 + 6 + 7 + 8 + 9
scala> val evenNums = r filter { x => x %2 == 0 } // 1
evenNums: scala.collection.immutable.Stream[Int] = Stream(0, ?)
```

We are jumping the gun a bit here. We are using filter, a functional combinator. We will be taking a detailed look at combinators in a next chapter. Refer to the following information box for a quick introduction.

```
scala> val p = List(1,2,3,4)
p: List[Int] = List(1, 2, 3, 4)
scala> p filter { x => x > 2 }
res40: List[Int] = List(3, 4)
```

The filter is called on the list p. Filter takes as argument a function. This function returns a Boolean, that is, the function is a predicate. It runs every element through the function, and **filters out elements** for which the function returns false. The result is **a new list**. Remember we are in the no-mutation side of the world. The original list, p, is left untouched and is persistent.

A still shorter form of the filter combinator uses the place holder syntax:

```
scala> p filter { _ > 2 }
```

which allows us to leave the parameter unnamed.

Let's check the following line:

```
scala> p filter { _ > 2 }
res41: List[Int] = List(3, 4)
```

We don't really need to name the element. The shorter form refers to the element via a _ .

Also note that we don't need to put `.` to qualify the method call. The following are equivalent:

```
scala> p filter { _ > 2 }
res41: List[Int] = List(3, 4)
scala> p.filter { _ > 2 }
res42: List[Int] = List(3, 4)
```

Pattern matching also works as expected:

```
scala> lazy val r = t(1)
r: Stream[Int] = <lazy>
scala> r match {
     |     case 1 #:: 2 #:: _ => println("match")
     | }
match
```

Sieve of Eratosthenes

Star gazing at night—we sometimes wonder—How many stars are there in the universe? How many galaxies? How many natural numbers are there? All these are really not finite. They are infinite! Prime numbers are also infinite. A brilliant algorithm to find prime numbers was found by Eratosthenes of Cyrene, a Greek mathematician. Named after him, the Sieve of Eratosthenes algorithm can be very nicely expressed as follows:

```
scala> def numStream(n: Int): Stream[Int] =
     | Stream.from(n) // 1
numStream: (n: Int)Stream[Int]
scala> def sieve(stream: Stream[Int]): Stream[Int] =
     |    stream.head #:: sieve((stream.tail) filter (x => x % stream.head
!= 0)) // 2
sieve: (stream: Stream[Int])Stream[Int]
scala> val p = sieve(numStream(2))
p: Stream[Int] = Stream(2, ?)
scala> (p take 5) foreach { println(_) }
2
3
5
7
11
```

By dissecting the code, we get the following findings:

1. We have a stream that generates successive numbers, starting off from the argument. We create the stream using the `Stream.form()` method:

2. The `sieve` is a method that takes a number stream. It lazily generates successive elements by filtering out any elements.

Let's grok this business. The following is a complete code:

```scala
object Sieve extends App {
  def f(s: Stream[Int], head: Int) = { // 1
    val r = s filter {
      x => {
        if (x % head != 0) {
          println(s"${x} is not evenly divisible by ${head}")
          true   // 2
        } else {
          println(s"${x} is evenly divisible by ${head}")
          println(s"Discarding ${x}")
          false // 3
        }
      }
    }
    r  // 4
  }

  def numStream(n: Int): Stream[Int] =
    Stream.from(n)

  def sieve(stream: Stream[Int]): Stream[Int] =
    stream.head #:: sieve(f(stream.tail, stream.head)) // 5

  val p = sieve(numStream(2))

  (p take 5) foreach { // driver
    println(_)
  }
}
```

Running it, we get the following output:

```
2

3 is not evenly divisible by 2

3
```

```
4 is evenly divisible by 2
Discarding 4
5 is not evenly divisible by 2
5 is not evenly divisible by 3
5
6 is evenly divisible by 2
Discarding 6
7 is not evenly divisible by 2
7 is not evenly divisible by 3
7 is not evenly divisible by 5
7
8 is evenly divisible by 2
Discarding 8
9 is not evenly divisible by 2
9 is evenly divisible by 3
Discarding 9
10 is evenly divisible by 2
Discarding 10
11 is not evenly divisible by 2
11 is not evenly divisible by 3
11 is not evenly divisible by 5
11 is not evenly divisible by 7
11
```

The following is a diagram:

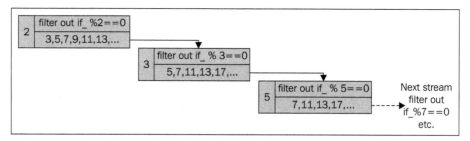

Figure 4.8: Stream wrapping another stream

We define a method `f()` that inserts debugging statements in the `filter` method.

When the stream finds a good element, that is, which is not evenly divisible by the head, we print it and return true.

Otherwise, we print the filtering out sequence. Note that when an element is discarded by a stream, it is not seen by a downstream one.

Finally, we return the stream.

The `sieve` method is modified to use the stream creation method, `f`.

As earlier, the driver takes off elements from our recursive stream and prints it.

Try playing with it by extending the diagram to see what happens when we advance to 7 (it is a prime number and hence selected).

Try to visualize why 8, 9, and 10 are discarded. The next number produced is 11, which is again a prime number.

A view to a collection

Databases have views. A database view works just like a table; however, the table never exists. It is just an illusion. A view is only a stored query, which is run when the view name is referenced:

```
Mysql> CREATE VIEW first_last AS SELECT first_name, last_name FROM NAMES
WHERE last_name LIKE ('k%');
mysql> SELECT first_name FROM first_last;
```

The `view first_last` query is backed by the result set of a query, on a real table, `NAMES`. We can select only the columns of interest and apply some **transformations** on them.

Scala collection views are similar. We will soon be giving a close look to **functional transformation**. However, to get a taste, the following is an example:

We need to assign a temporary password to a user. We have a list of randomly generated passwords. We need to pick one.

Our validation rules are:

1. A password cannot be empty.
2. It must have at least an uppercase letter.
3. It should have a numeric character.
4. It must have a special character.
5. It must have five or more characters.

We cobble together some transformations:

```scala
scala> val p = List("", "9#greaT", "is great", "greater", "23#pp",
"Aa#@4")


p: List[String] = List("", 9#greaT, is great, greater, 23#pp, Aa#@4)


scala> p filterNot (_.isEmpty) filter (_.exists(_.isDigit)) filter
(_.exists(_.isUpper)) filter (_.matches( """^.*[\W].*$""")) filter
(_.length >= 5)


res2: List[String] = List(9#greaT, Aa#@4)
```

The problem is that each filter is creating an intermediate list. This is in keeping with what we are saying. We never change the list in place. Lists are immutable! Remember our discussion on immutability and persistent data structures? The following is how the transformation looks:

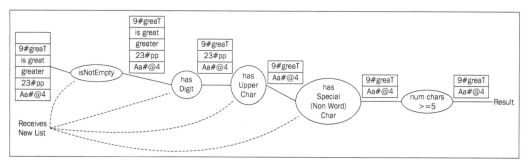

Figure 4.9: The transformation pipeline

We can convert all these transformations to be applied lazily:

```scala
scala> val v = p.view


v: scala.collection.SeqView[String,List[String]] = SeqView(...)
scala> val pv = v.filterNot(_.isEmpty).filter (_.exists(_.isDigit)).
filter (_.exists(_.isUpper)).filter (_.matches( """^.*[\W].*$""")).filter
(_.length >= 5)


pv: scala.collection.SeqView[String,List[String]] = SeqViewFFFFF(...)
scala> val x = pv.take(1)


x: scala.collection.SeqView[String,List[String]] = SeqViewFFFFFS(...)
```

```
scala> x.force
```

```
res7: List[String] = List(9#greaT)
```

```
scala>
```

We use a **force** call to convert the non-strict list of element 1 to a strict list. Strict data structures are evaluated completely. Non-strict ones are evaluated on a need basis.

Note all FFFFFs when we define pv? The filter functions are stored and applied all at once when we try to get at the first element.

The following is a version with trace statements that will help in understanding the flow:

```
scala> def working(s: String) = println(s"Working on ${s}")
scala> def isEmpty(s: String) = {
     |    working(s)
     |    s.isEmpty
     | }
scala> def hasOneDigit(s: String) = {
     |    working(s)
     |    s.exists(_.isDigit)
     | }
scala> def hasOneUpperCaseChar(s: String) = {
     |    working(s)
     |    s.exists(_.isUpper)
     | }
scala> def matches(s: String) = {
     |    working(s)
     |    s.matches( """^.*[\W].*$""")
     | }
scala> def hasMinLen(s: String) = {
     |    working(s)
     |    s.length >= 5
     | }
```

Now, have a look at the following statements:

```
scala> val pv = v.filterNot(isEmpty).filter(hasOneDigit).
filter(hasOneUpperCaseChar).filter(matches).filter(hasMinLen)
pv: scala.collection.SeqView[String,List[String]] = SeqViewFFFFF(...)

scala> val x = pv.take(4)
x: scala.collection.SeqView[String,List[String]] = SeqViewFFFFFS(...)

scala> x.force
Working on
Working on 9#greaT
Working on 9#greaT
Working on 9#greaT
Working on 9#greaT
Working on 9#greaT
```

All the filters are triggered on the first element. If the element satisfies all filters, it makes into the result list. There are no intermediate lists as in the strict evaluation.

When our input list is huge, not creating intermediate results could get us significant savings!

Summary

Lazy acquisition is a pretty commonly used pattern. The proxy design pattern is a nice example of Lazy Acquisition. ORM frameworks like Hibernate use proxies for lazy loading. Scala pushes the envelope by providing lazy vals and streams, which provide for on-demand computation, using thunks. Memoization is a related pattern to avoid computing the same value again. Instead, the value is cached. Java's autoboxing classes use memoization to conserve memory. Scala's streams use memoization and strike a balance between on-demand computation and memoization. Call by name is another powerful technique for delayed evaluation of code.

Let's now try mixing in some traits to our bag of Scala techniques in next chapters. Traits are Java interfaces and much more. Tighten your seat belts and let's deep dive into yet another of the powerful Scala features.

5
Taming Multiple Inheritance with Traits

When it is summer time in India and the heat is just unbearable, our hands instinctively reach out for either the AC remote or the regulator knob. And in a matter of minutes, we get bliss! An AC remote is pretty simple to operate and so is a ceiling fan regulator. A handful of push buttons that are easily understood by anyone. However, a remote is an interface. It is the system's way of allowing the external world to interact with it. A regulator knob is another, and so is a TV remote and the numeric keypad on your phone. As the air conditioner is a complex system, it needs to expose a simple way in which the consumer can use it. A motorbike too is a complex machine. You just need to know how to kick start it into life, change gears, and off you go. The bike also comes equipped with useful stuff, such as a fuel gauge and a speedometer. An AC remote, a bike fuel gauge, and a fan regulator are all interfaces. Think of a system and you will see an interface. Interfaces are everywhere!

Interfaces allow us, the external world, to help use complex systems. We cannot even imagine driving a car without essential interfaces such as a gear box and a speedometer. Interfaces are the touch points exposed by the system so that the world can use them.

Interfaces are also contracts. When you implement one, you need to meet the interface requirements. For example, the gear box of a car should work in the same way no matter what type of car it is. The speedometer should also work in the same way for all the cars. Interfaces provide a warranty for the caller (also known as the external world), that the class implementing an interface can do some operation, without knowing the internal details of exactly how it does the magic. A class can implement multiple interfaces. If it does so, it needs to abide by multiple contracts as well.

In this chapter, we will look at the iterator design pattern in Java to understand the contract aspect of interfaces better. We will also look at abstract classes and the template method. We will then see why Java forbids us from extending multiple abstract classes and shaking hands with the dreaded diamond. Armed with all this knowledge, we will look at Scala traits. Traits are similar to Java interfaces, and with more and some more features. Traits allow mix-ins, a composition mechanism. Next, we will see what stackable traits are and get a taste of the cake pattern. Finally, we will come to know about the linearization mechanism. This is how Scala defeats the dreaded diamond. Let's get on to it!

The iterator design pattern

Surfing channels on a TV acts as a stress buster for me. Switching channels back and forth is so soothing. This process of visiting channels in an order is called iteration. When we are in a hotel room, away from home, the aired channels may be different. However, the process of iteration remains the same. We visit a channel, we may spend some time watching it, and if we feel bored again, we go to the next one.

In programming, visiting each element of a data structure is routinely required. To make itself iterable, the data structures produce an iterator object. The iterator object needs to obey a contract that is laid down by the interface. For example, if the data structure produces an instance of `java.lang.Iterable`, then we can use Java's `foreach` loop to visit each element, that is, we can iterate the data structure. Let's look at the following figure:

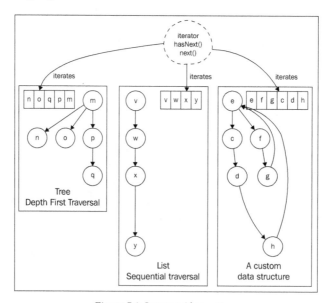

Figure 5.1: Iterator Abstraction

The following Java code snippet shows how we can iterate various data structures. Java's `foreach` loop can iterate our custom data structures as it obeys the `iterable` contract:

```java
// generic class to print elements
package chapter05;
public class PrintElems {
  public void print(Iterable<Integer> iterator) {
    System.out.println(""--- Start ---"");
    for (Integer i : iterator) { // 1
      System.out.println(i);
    }
    System.out.println(""--- End ---"");
  }
}
// Our own iterator implementation
package chapter05;
import java.util.Iterator;

public class MyDataStruct {
  public Iterable<Integer> values() {
    return new Iterable<Integer>() {
      private final int[] array = new int[]{ 5, 11, 22 };
      @Override
      public Iterator<Integer> iterator() {
        return new Iterator<Integer>() {

          private int i = 0;

          @Override
          public boolean hasNext() { // 2
            return i != array.length;
          }

          @Override
          public Integer next() {
            return array[i++]; // 3
          }
          // remove method not shown
        };
      }
    };
  }
}
```

```
/////// Driver.java
package chapter05;

import java.util.Map;

import com.google.common.collect.Lists;
import com.google.common.collect.Maps;
import com.google.common.collect.Sets;

public class Driver {
  public static void main(String[] args) {
    Map<String, Integer> lhmap = Maps.newLinkedHashMap();
    lhmap.put(""one"", 1);
    lhmap.put(""two"", 2);
    lhmap.put(""three"", 3);

    PrintElems pe = new PrintElems();
    pe.print(lhmap.values());

    pe.print(Maps.newHashMap(lhmap).values()); // 4

    pe.print(Sets.newHashSet((lhmap).values())); // 5

    pe.print(Lists.newArrayList((lhmap).values())); // 6

    MyDataStruct p = new MyDataStruct();

    pe.print(p.values()); // 7
  }
}
```

In the preceding code, both java.util.Set and java.util.Map are interfaces. Here, we are creating HashSet and HashMap. The data structure that we've used internally is a hash table. A java.util.ArrayList uses arrays. There is one more implementation, java.util.LinkedList. This one uses a linked list internally. Both of these implement the java.util.List interface. LinkedHashMap extends the HashMap data structure. It uses an additional data structure, a doubly linked list. This list keeps track of the insertion order. Note that the LinkedHashMap output is in the same order in which we inserted the entries.

We use another technique, that is, programming to an interface. When I program to an interface, I just need the functionality. I don't care where it comes from! When I just care about the functionality, I can plug in various providers without affecting the code that uses them.

So, we need to avoid using the following code:

```
private ArrayList<Integer> someList;
public ArrayList getAList() {
    return someList; // 1
}
```

And instead of using the preceding code, we should always use the code given here:

```
public List getAList() {
        return someList; // 2
}
```

The advantage of the second form is that we can easily replace one implementation of the interface with another, as shown in the following code:

```
public List getAList() {
        return Collections.unmodifiable(someList);
}
```

That is **just one line of code change**. Now, we are going to expose a **read-only** list so that no one can tamper with our **class invariants**.

Refer to http://people.cs.aau.dk/~normark/oop-csharp/ html/notes/contracts_themes-class-inv-sect.html for more information on class invariants.

The salient points of the preceding code are as follows:

- The `PrintElems.print(...)` method uses the `java.lang.Iterable` interface as a type. We need to send an argument that implements `Iterable`; otherwise, the code won't be compiled.

- Next, we implement the `Iterator` interface. In order to satisfy the contract, one of the methods that we need to implement is `hasNext`. This is used to know whether there are any more elements that are left to be traversed.

- Similarly, the next method yields the next element. Our internal data is just an array. However, the client code using the iterator does not know and care about such details. This is an example of encapsulation.

- Then, we exercise the `PrintElems.print(...)` method by creating `java.util.HashMap`. This class provides a `values()` method, which is an iterator. The `values()` method returns a collection that implements `Iterable`.

- After this, we use `java.util.HashSet`, which implements the `java.util.Set` interface. Sets, too, implement the `Iterable` interface. `HashSet` obeys the contract and provides a suitable `values()` method, which returns `Iterable`.

- Then, we create `java.util.ArrayList`, which implements the `java.util.List` interface. As the `List` interface extends the `Iterable` interface, the contract is obeyed by `ArrayList`. Then, we get `Iterable`.

- We pass in our `Iterable` data structure. which extends the `Iterable` interface, the `printElems` can use the `foreach` loop on it too.

The `Iterable` interface specifies a contract. Any class implementing it promises to provide appropriate `hasNext()` and `next()` methods. The print method of `PrintElems` does not really know or care what the data structure really is. The `foreach` loop exclusively uses the `Iterable` interface to visit each element.

Interfaces as types

Interfaces specify only what a class can do (or which contracts it obeys) and not how the class does this. On the other hand, non-related classes can share some common behavior. If we somehow could write this behavior in one place, we would be following the **Don't Repeat Yourself principle (DRY)**.

The DRY principle aims at reducing repetition. We can look at a method, a function, or a class as a piece of knowledge. This means that a function or method knows how to do something. The principle tells us not to duplicate this know-how.

It is easier to change this one piece or replace it with another, as this won't affect other logically unrelated elements. Brian Kernighan, the legendary programmer, calls this the **Single Point Of Truth (SPOT)** principle.

Refer to `http://www.linuxtopia.org/online_books/programming_books/art_of_unix_programming/ch04s02_2.html` for more on this important design principle.

Let's try the following code as an example of an interface:

```
// NameIt.java
public interface NameIt {
  public String name();
}
// GoodsMover.java
public interface GoodsMover extends NameIt {
  void moveGoods();
}
// Walks.java
public interface Walks extends NameIt {
```

```
    public void walk();
  }
  // Donkey.java
  public class Donkey implements Walks, GoodsMover, NameIt {
    public void walk() {
      ProcessIt.walk(this);
    }
    public void moveGoods() {
      ProcessIt.moveGoods(this);
    }
    public String name() {
      return ""Donkey"";
    }
  }
  // Horse.java
  public class Horse implements Walks, NameIt {
    public void walk() {
      ProcessIt.walk(this);
    }
    public String name() {
      return ""Horse"";
    }
  }
  // Driver.java
  public class Driver {
    public static void main(String[] args) {
      Horse horse = new Horse();
      Donkey donkey = new Donkey();
      donkey.walk();
      donkey.moveGoods();
      horse.walk();
    }
  }
  // ProcessIt.java
  public class ProcessIt {
    public static void moveGoods(GoodsMover goodsMover){// 1
      System.out.println(goodsMover.name() + "" busy moving heavy
        stuff"");
    }
    public static void walk(Walks walker) { // 2
      System.out.println(walker.name() + "" is having a stroll now"");
    }
  }
```

Here is a UML diagram for the preceding example:

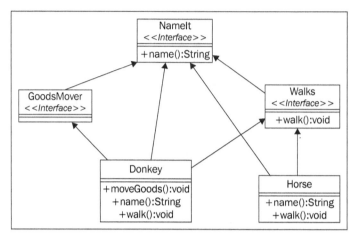

Figure 5.2: A UML diagram for the Animal hierarchy

The salient points for the interface example are as follows:

- The `moveGoods(GoodsMover goodsMover)` method uses the `GoodsMover` interface as a type

- Similarly, the `walk(Walks walker)` method uses the `Walks` interface as a type

Now, we want to write the `walk` method only once and use it for any walkers. However, we cannot write implementations in a Java interface. To share the implementation code of an interface method, we need to write auxiliary classes such as `ProcessIt`.

The dreaded diamond

Mules are hybrid animals. Charles Darwin found them most surprising. Mules possess more reason, memory, obstinacy, social affection, powers of muscular endurance, endurance, and length of life than either of their parents, namely donkey and horse.

Now, the question is how would we model mules in our system? Mules obviously walk and move goods. So, we might be tempted to model mules by extending both `Horse` and `Donkey`. Alas! We cannot! Java allows a class to extend from only one class — also known as a single inheritance. We don't wish to rewrite the `walk` and `moveGoods` methods again for mules. If the language allowed us to extend `mules` from both `Horse` and `Donkey`, it would be just the thing! Let's see the following diagrammatic representation for this example:

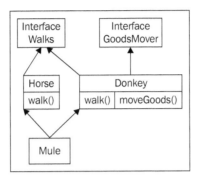

Figure 5.3: The dreaded diamond

The problem here is the **walk()** method. As the diagram shows, which walk method implementation would **Mule** inherit? Would it be the one from **Horse**? Or the one from **Donkey**?

You would think we are relying way too much on inheritance. Shouldn't we really favor composition over inheritance? Sure, point taken. However, we very much want to send a **Mule** object where the expected argument type is, **Walks**. If we favor composition, the compiler precisely won't allow us to do this.

"**Composition over inheritance**" is a core object-oriented programming principle. The design pattern's movement advocates favoring composition over inheritance. The bridge design pattern is an application of this idea. Say, you want to draw colored shapes. You won't define the patterns you've made as RedCircle, YellowEclipse, and BlueRectangle. Rather, you would define a shape hierarchy and a color hierarchy. You can then define an abstract color in a shape. In this case, a composition wins hands down! Composing a shape with color helps us tame a class explosion.

Refer to `https://www.thoughtworks.com/insights/blog/composition-vs-inheritance-how-choose for more on this theme` to see an example of composition over inheritance.

Traits – Scala's rich interfaces

It would be super cool if we could write reusable code as well as get rid of the dreaded diamond. Scala's traits is the answer if we want to do this.

Here is how we could implement the preceding hierarchy in Scala:

```scala
object RichInterfaces extends App {
  trait NameIt { // 1
    def name(): String // 2
  }
  trait Walks extends NameIt { // 3
    def walk() = // 4
    println(name() + "" is having a stroll now"")
  }
  trait GoodsMover extends NameIt {
  def moveGoods() =
    println(name() + "" busy moving heavy stuff"")
  }
  class Horse extends Walks { // 5
    override def name(): String = ""Horse""
  }
  class Donkey extends Walks with GoodsMover { // 6
    override def name(): String = ""Donkey""
  }

  val horse = new Horse
  val donkey = new Donkey

  horse.walk() // 7
  donkey.walk()
  donkey.moveGoods()
}
```

The salient points of the preceding code are as follows:

- In the code, we defined a `NameIt` trait. This is very similar to a Java interface
- We then declared a `name()` method, again, in Java interfaces
- After this, the `Walks` trait extends the `NameIt` trait

- The `Walks` trait then defines the reusable `walk()` method implementation

- The `Horse` class mixes in the `Walks` trait

- The `Donkey` class then mixes in the `Walks` and `GoodsMover` traits

- After this, we call `horse.walk()` that executes the `walk()` method defined in `Walks` trait

Look again at the `walk()` method of the `Walks` trait. Earlier, in the Java implementation, we had to provide an implementation that just delegated to the `ProcessIt` class. In the Scala solution, we could add this same code as a concrete method in the trait itself.

Our `NameIt` trait has a thin interface. `NameIt` is mixed into `Walks` and `GoodsMover`, as both have concrete methods and a rich interface.

 Rich interfaces do more work by themselves, so the clients (`Horse`, `Donkey`) need to write less code. On the other hand, thin interfaces make clients write more code to implement them. Needless to say, Java interfaces are thin, as they made us write more code. We had to implement `walk()` and `moveGoods()` to implement the interfaces.

You can mix in traits with an object too. Let's go to the REPL and try the following command to do so:

```
scala> import RichInterfaces._
import RichInterfaces._
scala> val gmHorse = new Horse with GoodsMover
gmHorse: RichInterfaces.Horse with RichInterfaces.GoodsMover =
$anon$1@1cc7580f
scala>    gmHorse.moveGoods
Horse busy moving heavy stuff
scala> val h = new Horse
h: RichInterfaces.Horse = RichInterfaces$Horse@3f1d2e23
scala> h.moveGoods
<console>:13: error: value moveGoods is not a member of RichInterfaces.
Horse
              h.moveGoods
              ^
```

Here, we created `Horse` and `gmHorse`, and we gave it good moving powers. As `h` is a normal horse, it won't move goods for you!

Our mules can be created as shown in the following code:

```scala
scala>    val mule = (new Walks with GoodsMover {
     |       override def name(): String = ""Mule""
     |    })
mule: RichInterfaces.Walks with RichInterfaces.GoodsMover =
$anon$1@4823400e
scala>    mule.walk()
Mule is having a stroll now
scala>    mule.moveGoods()
Mule busy moving heavy stuff
scala>
```

The `mule` method points to an anonymous object with the traits attached to it.

Mix-ins – rich interfaces

Let's add a funny twist to the tale. We will now remove the `NameIt` trait and change both the traits, as shown in the following code:

```scala
trait Walks {
  def name : String
  def walk() =
    println(name + "" is having a stroll now"")
}
trait GoodsMover {
  def name : String
  def moveGoods() =
    println(name + "" busy moving heavy stuff"")
}
```

The `name()` method, referred to by the traits, must be defined somewhere. As long as `Horse` and `Donkey` define the `name()` method, it works.

Writing a rating comparison algorithm for our animals illustrates one major use of the traits. Our rating is a simple number. Try the following snippet to implement the `compare` method:

```scala
object CompareAnimals extends App {
  // traits Walks and GoodsMover not shown
```

```
    abstract class Animal(val rating: Int) extends Ordered[Animal]

    class Horse(rating: Int) extends Animal(rating) with Walks { // 1
      override def name(): String = ""Horse""
      override def compare(that: Animal): Int = rating - that.rating //
2
    }

    class Donkey(rating: Int) extends Animal(rating) with Walks with
GoodsMover {
      override def name(): String = ""Donkey""
      override def compare(that: Animal): Int = rating - that.rating
    }
    val horse = new Horse(1)
    val donkey = new Donkey(2)
    if (horse < donkey) { // 3
      println(""Donkeys are more useful than horses - breed Donkeys"")
    } else if (horse > donkey) {
      println(""Horses are more useful than donkeys - breed Horses"")
    }
    // we don''t get == though
}
```

The salient points for the preceding code are as follows:

- Here, we are using the standard ordered trait. This trait forces us to implement the compare method.

- The `compare` method returns 0 if the objects are equal, negative if the receiver is less than the argument, and positive otherwise.

- We have not defined any < method in the code. The ordered trait has enriched our interface by defining the < method in terms of the `compare` method that we provided.

More fun awaits us.

Frills and thrills – the decorator pattern

We need to add the functionality whereby animals get inoculated by a vet. Also, an animal should be inoculated only once. In practice, we would normally inoculate them at intervals. However, we simplify things to make our point. We want to wrap the logic "*if already inoculated, then skip*" without touching the animal code. The decorator pattern now comes to our rescue.

A decorator is a design pattern that wraps an object. It mimics the interface of the object that it is decorating. Here is the Java code in which we will look at how Scala makes the pattern easy and breezy.

The Java listing here has just the necessary changes. Refer to the book source code for the complete listing:

```java
public class AnimalDecorator extends Animal { // 1
  protected Animal animal; // 2
  public AnimalDecorator(Animal animal) {
    this.animal = animal;
  }
  public void getInoculated() {
    animal.getInoculated(); // 3 // delegate to next decorator
    // or animal
  }
  @Override
    public boolean isAlreadyInnoculated() {
      return animal.isAlreadyInnoculated(); // 4
    }
  @Override
    public String name() {
      return animal.name();
    }
}
public class SkipIfInnoculated extends AnimalDecorator {
  // constructor code not shown...
  public void getInoculated() { // 5
    System.out.println("Checking if decorated");
    if (animal.isAlreadyInnoculated()) {
      System.out.println(name() + " already ioculated -
        Skipping");
  } else {
      super.getInoculated();
    }
  }
  // Driver.java
  public static void main(String[] args) {
    Horse horse = new Horse();
    Doctor doctor = new Vet();
    horse.setDoctor(doctor); // inject the doctor dependency
    AnimalDecorator decoratedHorse = new SkipIfInnoculated(new
    InnoculateAnimal(horse)); // 6 // horse with frills
    decoratedHorse.getInoculated(); // outputs message
    decoratedHorse.getInoculated(); // skips inoculation
    }
```

The salient points of the preceding code are as follows:

- The `Animal Decorator` class is completely substitutable (it is an animal).
- However, it is just a wrapper. It does its bit and delegates to the real stuff—which could be a decorator again.
- Then, the `getInoculated()` call gets delegated.
- The Boolean status if the `animal` is already inoculated. Note that this call is really satisfied by the actual animal (`horse` in the example case).
- This is the logic that we need to execute. Skip inoculation if the animal is already inoculated.
- The decorator is created by composing other decorators and the target object.
- The crux to understand the preceding example is to know that each method call is terminated at the target object.

Here is a UML diagram that shows you how the classes relate to each other:

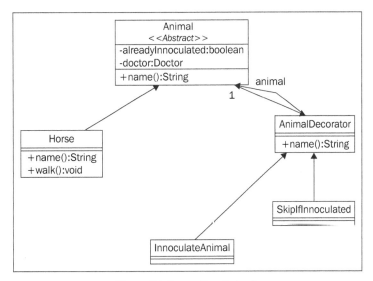

Figure 5.4: Decorating Animals

Scala's easy and breezy decorations – stackable modifications

As we know well by now, programming in Scala is super simple. Actually, this is one major use of traits, namely to modify the existing class methods of an object. I am just giving the new methods now. You can refer to the following sample code for a working example:

```scala
abstract class Animal(val rating: Int) {
  def giveInoculation(): Unit  // abstract method
  def alreadyInoculated() : Boolean // abstract method
}
trait FilterOutAlreadyInoculated extends Animal {
  abstract override def giveInoculation(): Unit = // 1
    if (!alreadyInoculated())
      super.giveInoculation()
}
class Horse(rating: Int, var inoculated: Boolean = false) extends
Animal(rating) with Walks with Ordered[Animal] {
...

  override def giveInoculation(): Unit = {
    println(name() + "" Getting inoculated"")
    inoculated = true
  }
  override def alreadyInoculated(): Boolean = inoculated
}
```

```
Going to the REPL:
scala> import Stackable._
scala> val horse = new Horse(1) with FilterOutAlreadyInoculated
...   // mix in the filtering trait
scala> horse.giveInoculation // invoke
Horse Getting inoculated
scala> horse.giveInoculation
// Nothing printed here
```

The `abstract override` method tells the compiler that the trait sporting it must be mixed into a class that has a concrete definition.

The trait intercepts the `giveInoculation()` method on the object, and if it is already inoculated, the inoculation is skipped. Here is the diagrammatic representation of this example:

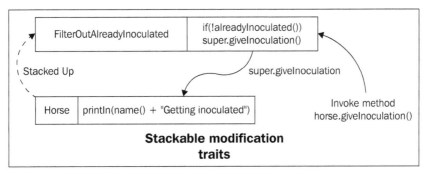

Figure 5.5: Stackable modifications

What do we mean by the term stackable? Let's introduce another trait, nullifying the filter, as shown in the following code:

```
trait NullifyFiltering extends Animal {
    override def alreadyInoculated() = false
}
scala> val horse = new Horse(1) with NullifyFiltering with
FilterOutAlreadyInoculated
...
scala> horse.giveInoculation
Horse Getting inoculated
scala> horse.giveInoculation
Horse Getting inoculated
```

The `alreadyInoculated()` method in `horse` is not called. Rather, the `NullifyFiltering`'s `alreadyInoculated()` method is called! This sets back the flag to `false`, so the `if` condition in the filtering trait is never true! Refer to the following figure of call order to understand this:

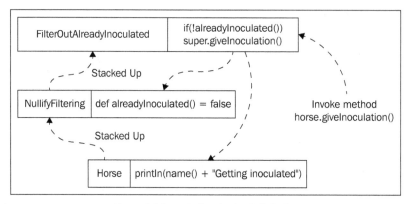

Figure6: Mix-in Left to Right Call Order

Dependencies injection pattern

The Hollywood principle (https://en.wikipedia.org/wiki/Hollywood_principle) is stated as *"don't call us, we'll call you"*. One might hear this response after auditioning for a role in a movie. It won't work if the candidates call the recruiting agency every day. The agency would get swamped with calls if there were many candidates.

Instead, the agency will call back if they find someone suitable and want to take it forward.

This **Inversion Of Control (IoC)** applies to software designs too. IoC is different from other more traditional forms of programming.

Refer to https://techbizcurry.wordpress.com/2014/04/07/hollywood-principle-inversion-of-control-design-pattern/ for an excellent explanation.

Here is a real-world scenario. Test-first development advocates writing tests before you write the production code. Following this advice makes for better code, as it gives us a test harness. A test harness, in turn, would make us more confident in refactoring the code base and help us keep it clean.

The advice seems a little odd though. Surely, programming by intention (refer to the following example) helps, but what about collaborators of an object? Any class object typically works in tandem with other objects.

> Programming by intention is a productivity booster technique that is used while you are cutting code. This is one major benefit of using IDEs such as Eclipse and IntelliJ. For example, in our Java version, you can express your intention by writing the following code:
>
> ```
> Mule mule = new Mule();
> ```
>
> As there is no `Mule` class present, the compiler complains. In Eclipse, you see a red mark indicating the error. Now, pressing *Ctrl + 1*, the quick fix shortcut, Eclipse pops up a suggestion to fix this error. The suggestion is "**Create class "Mule"**". By clicking on this, Eclipse guides you to the class creation.
>
> Next, really want to read the preceding line as:
>
> ```
> Animal animal = new Mule();
> ```
>
> Again, you will see the red mark. For quick fixing, we choose a suggestion to create the `Animal` interface. However, `Mule` still does not implement `Animal`. Quick fixing allows us to "**Let "Mule" implement "Animal"**".
>
> You can create missing class methods in this way. You implement interface contract methods too via quick fix. I don't remember the last time I coded a method itself. This quick fix is one great reason to start using an IDE.

Now, our animals will have an owner. The owner is a person who, in turn, will have collaborators such as an address. Animals will also have a caretaker, who is yet another person. The caretaker too will have an address collaborator object. Animals also have an associated doctor. You get the idea, right? We rarely deal with single objects. We instead deal with object graphs!

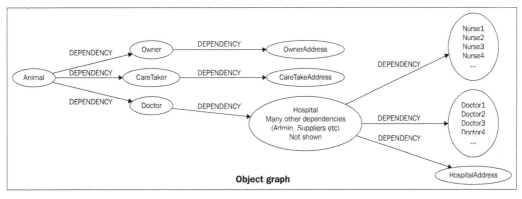

Figure 5.7: An animal objects graph

These collaborators, such as the **Owner** for an **Animal** is a dependency. When asked the name of its owner, the animal, in turn, needs to ask the owner. Similarly, to fulfill the **"get inoculated"** message, the **Animal** needs to depend on the **Doctor** dependency.

So far, so good. Now, suppose that we need to create the dependencies at construction time:

```
Animal() {
   this.doctor = new Doctor(); // Coupling

   // … initialization of other members
}
```

The problem with this code is that the Animal's `doctor` field is hard wired to the `Doctor` class. In other words, the `doctor` field is tightly coupled with the `Doctor` class. However, we are violating one important mantra here. The systems should now have loose coupling and high cohesion.

Why? One reason for this is that we cannot test this easily. More specifically, we need to develop the `Doctor` class first (which could be fairly complicated itself as it will need its own collaborator and hospital defined first) and then only we can reliably construct `Animal`. The test-first paradigm tells us to write tests before we write any production code. Quite a chicken and egg situation!

The other reason is that we would want the `Hospital`, `Doctor`, and `Animal` classes to evolve separately. The way out is to first perform extract interface refactoring. Refer to `http://www.refactoring.com/catalog/extractInterface.html` for more information on refactoring.

Secondly, we can use the **test double** technique, namely a **mock object**. Refer to `http://xunitpatterns.com/Test%20Double.html` and `http://martinfowler.com/articles/mocksArentStubs.html` for more information.

I am showing only the relevant changes here. The book source code has the complete example. Take a look at the changes in the following example:

```
Public interface Doctor {
  void noculate(Animal animal);
}
public abstract class Animal {
  private Doctor doctor;
  public void getInoculated() {
    doctor.innoculate(this);
```

```
  }
  public void setDoctor(Doctor doctor) {
    this.doctor = doctor;
  }
}
public class AnimalsTest {
  @Test
  public void testInnoculation() {
    Doctor doctor = mock(Doctor.class); // 1
    Animal animal = new Horse();
    animal.setDoctor(doctor); // 2
    animal.getInoculated();

    verify(doctor).innoculate(animal); // 3
  }
}
```

The salient points of the preceding code are as follows:

- We create the test double, also known as The mock.
- We set the doctor dependency of the animal object to the mock object, which was created in the line labeled as 1.
- We verified the expectation that the mock method, getInoculated(), was invoked.

 We are using a popular mocking library, Mockito (http://mockito. org/). Other popular mock libraries, powermock and jMock are available too. We can define a mock and inject it as a dependency for the class under test. We use the setter injection (that is, call the setter method) and verify that the expectations are met.

The crux is that instead of the animal controlling which dependency to use, we control it from the outside. This, again, is IoC. Dependency injection is a form of IoC.

Spring is a great DI framework. We write code in the form of beans. Beans are Spring-managed objects. We configure beans in an application context and you can wire up bean dependencies using XML or Java annotations. For example:

```
@Component
public class Animal {
   @Autowire
   private Doctor doctor;
   ...
}
```

The `Animal` is a Spring-managed bean indicated by the `@Component` annotation. `Animal` has a `Doctor` dependency. We express the dependency using the `@Autowire` annotation. Spring finds a `Doctor` bean (a Spring-managed Java object) and injects the bean as a dependency via a setter injection, that is, Spring invokes the `Animal`'s `setDoctor(Doctor doctor)` method.

In Scala, we can use the cake pattern to inject dependencies.

A taste of the cake pattern

Scala provides a nice way to inject dependencies via a feature called **self-annotation**. This is useful to inject dependencies. Consider the `giveInnoculation()` method in `Animal`, as shown here:

```
object ScalaDepInj extends App {

  abstract class Animal(val rating: Int, var inoculated:
  Boolean = false) {
    def name(): String

    def alreadyInoculated() = inoculated

    def setInoculated(b: Boolean) = {
      inoculated = b
    }
  }


  trait Vet { // 1
```

```scala
  def name(): String

  def inoculate(animal: Animal) = {
    println(""Innoculating "" + animal.name)
  }
}
trait ChoosyVet extends Vet { // 2
  def alreadyInoculated(): Boolean

  abstract override def inoculate(animal: Animal) = {
    if (!alreadyInoculated()) // filter out already
    // inoculated animals
      println(""Innoculating "" + animal.name)
  }
}

trait Inoculate {
  this: Animal with Vet => // 3
  def setInoculated(b: Boolean)

  def giveInoculation() = {
    inoculate(this)
    setInoculated(true)
  }

  def name(): String
}

class Horse(rating: Int) extends Animal(rating) {
  override def name(): String = ""Horse""
}

// driver
```

```
val h = new Horse(1) with ChoosyVet with Inoculate // 4

h.giveInoculation() // prints message
h.giveInoculation() // filtered out
}
```

Here is the diagrammatic representation of this example:

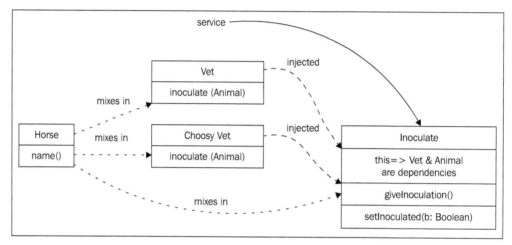

Figure 5.8: The Scalaish dependency injection

The salient points of this example are as follows:

- Here, we move the inoculation logic into a `Vet` trait
- We then define another `Vet` trait, `ChoosyVet`, which filters out the already inoculated animals
- This is a self-annotation. The **Inoculate** trait depends on a `Vet` trait
- We are mixing in a `ChoosyVet` trait, which skips the already inoculated animals

Try replacing `ChoosyVet` with `Vet` and check the output.

Why the pattern name has a cake? Cakes have many ingredients and you can add many more to get a unique flavor. We can use traits to configure the objects the way we want. Secondly, cakes have layers. Our traits are layered up too. This is the reason why.

Sealed traits

A trait can be sealed, meaning it can be extended only in the same file in which it is declared. Sealed traits are useful as the compiler can do **exhaustiveness** checks. What does being exhaustive mean? It is pretty simple. Try out the following example to know more:

```scala
scala> def m(n : Int) = n < 10
m: (n: Int)Boolean
scala> :t m _
Int => Boolean
scala> m(9) match {
     |    case true => println(""True"")
     | }
<console>:12: warning: match may not be exhaustive.
It would fail on the following input: false
       m(9) match {
         ^
True
```

The compiler can reason about the pattern match. It knows that the return type of m is `Boolean`. Note that we are calling the method and matching the result against `true`. What if the method returns `false`? This is the reason a cautionary warning is issued.

If we include the `false` clause, the warning would go away, as the code **would never fail to match**.

Let's take a look at another example in which we are matching against the `Option` type:

```scala
scala> val p = Option(1)
p: Option[Int] = Some(1)

scala> p match {
     |    case Some(x) => ""Ok""
     | }
<console>:9: warning: match may not be exhaustive.
It would fail on the following input: None
              p match {
                ^
res1: String = Ok
```

We have missed the `case` clause for `None`. How is the compiler able to do this?

Let's run to REPL and try out the following commands. Here, note that most of the output is elided to save space:

```
object SealedTraits extends App {
  trait Num // 1
  final case class One() extends Num
  final case class Two() extends Num
  p match {
    case _: One => println(""1"")
  }
}
```

```
%>  scalac SealedTraits.scala
// look ma, no warning!
```

Now, change the line labeled as 1 with the following:

```
sealed trait Num
```

```
Just tack on the sealed keyword before trait.
```

By recompiling the preceding code, we will get:

```
% scalac SealedTraits.scala
```

The `SealedTraits.scala:11: warning`: match may not be exhaustive.

The match would fail on the following input:

```
Two()
  p match {
    ^
```

```
one warning found
```

What happens when we tack on the `sealed` keyword? A sealed trait can only be extended within the file in which it is defined. The compiler can use this to perform exhaustiveness checking. Another idiom related to sealed traits is to provide an alternative to enums. And as we know, Java has enums.

Refer to `https://docs.oracle.com/javase/tutorial/java/javaOO/enum.html` for more information on enum types.

We can implement enums in Scala using the sealed traits, as shown in the following code:

```
object ScalaEnum extends App {
  sealed trait WeekDay
  case object Sun extends WeekDay
  case object Mon extends WeekDay
  case object Tue extends WeekDay
  case object Wed extends WeekDay
  case object Thu extends WeekDay
  case object Fri extends WeekDay
  case object Sat extends WeekDay

  def m(p: WeekDay) = println(p)

  m(Sat) // prints Sat
}
```

Here, the case object is yet another idiom. It is used when there is no instance-specific state! It is a kind of a singleton.

In the preceding code, WeekDay is an algebraic data type. All values of the WeekDay type are finite (the sealed keyword). WeekDay is taken as a sum type as it can be characterized as the sum of all unique, enumerated values.

Let's consider another sum type, Month:

```
sealed trait Month
case object Jan extends Month
… // define Feb, Mar, Apr,..., Dec
```

The sum, in this case would be 7.

```
sealed case class WeekDayOfMonth( dayOfWeek: WeekDay,
month: Month) // 1
```

Here, WeekDayOfMonth is a product type. And the number of WeekDayOfMonth instances is $7*12 = 84.$

The algebraic data type is a pure data type, and only wraps some values of other data types.

The line labeled as 1 is a value constructor. A value constructor just holds the values. Jan (that is, the month of January) is a case object here.

You can now define only a restricted number of instances of the class, WeekDayOfMonth, namely 84.

Defeating the dreaded diamond

We saw that the diamond prevented us from reusing the code. In C++ though, you can use **Multiple inheritance (MI)**, as it is sparingly used. In Java, you cannot use MI at all. In Scala, what happens when we mix in traits with two or more traits that have the same method? We saw earlier that the rightmost trait method gets called.

Here, there is an elaborate process, **linearization**, that flattens out the hierarchy. The process is described in all its nitty-gritty detail in the code labeled as 1. The mechanism effectively results in a single-method resolution. This avoids the method ambiguity, also known as, the dreaded diamond.

You get to reuse an implementation, add dependencies, and stack up behaviors in this method. This is an incredibly powerful way to design loosely coupled code. And we never ever have to fear the dreaded diamond rearing its head.

Summary

We had a pretty detailed look at Java interfaces and got to know that interfaces are contracts. When a class implements the contract, we can reuse the existing code. The iterator pattern is an example of such a contract. By following the interface iterable's contract, we were able to reuse the Java code for each loop with our own custom class.

When a language supports multiple inheritances, the method resolution might get ambiguous. Java does not support multiple inheritance, hence, we don't see this problem.

Scala traits resolve many of these problems. We can put in reusable code in traits and then mix-in traits into our classes or objects as needed. We looked at how mix-ins enable rich interfaces. Traits are stackable and allow us to change the existing object methods, namely stackable modifications.

Dependencies injection is a very popular pattern. The general theme behind it is inversion of control. Scala traits allow us to come up with their own dependencies injection and the cake pattern. Lastly, you learned about the pure algebraic data types and how to implement them in Scala.

The stage is pretty well set, dear reader, to tinker more and learn about currying and closures. Currying is a fundamental tenet of the functional way of things. Let's get on to it!

6
Currying Favors with Your Code

The word "curry" perks me up. The heavenly aromas wafting from the kitchen, the sheer magic worked out of legendary spices, and the right dash of salt—bliss! Life starts looking up again.

Scala, too, gives us constructs to liven up programming. We have used functions till now. However, in this chapter, we take a real good and close look at how easily we can pass around functions. We also look at some basic concepts such as lexical scopes and name binding. A discussion of local functions comes next. A discussion on closures comes after it. All these basics will help you to learn about two important techniques. The first is partially applied functions, with a nice detour into the intricacies of the underscore. The second exotic technique is currying. We will also look at some common currying usage. All this discussion lays down a nice groundwork on which patterns tread!

In this chapter, we will look at the loaner pattern, the template method design pattern, the java implementation and then the easy and breezy Scala version. Finally, we wrap up with a discussion on decorators and builders (again!) to see how these techniques make implementing these patterns super simple. And as usual, idioms and patterns are best learned by looking at code, so fire up the Scala REPL console, grab a cup of your favorite hot beverage, and off we go!

Functions as first-class values

Let's run to the REPL and try out the following command:

```
scala> val pred = (y: Int) => y < 10
pred: Int => Boolean = <function1>
```

The REPL here is saying that `pred` is a function (`<function1>`). Scala functions are first-class values. What does this term mean? We can send a first-class value as a parameter to another function, just like we send an integer, a list, or string.

For example, we can find the type of `pred` just like we can of `Int`:

```
scala> val q = 9
q: Int = 9
scala> :t q
Int
scala> :t pred
Int => Boolean
```

We can send the function `pred` to a function combinator, as shown in this code snippet:

```
scala> List(1,11,2,22,3,33) filter(pred)
res3: List[Int] = List(1, 2, 3)
```

We can send a function to another function and return a function from another function as follows:

```
scala> val pred1 = (y: Int) => y < 11 // 1
pred1: Int => Boolean = <function1>

scala> val higher: (Int => Boolean) => (Int => Boolean) = (k : Int =>
Boolean) => pred1 // 2
higher: (Int => Boolean) => (Int => Boolean) = <function1>

scala> val aFunc = higher(pred) // 3
aFunc: Int => Boolean = <function1>

scala> aFunc(12)
res4: Boolean = false

scala> aFunc(10)
res5: Boolean = true
```

The salient points for the preceding code are as follows:

- We define a function, `pred1`, that takes the parameter `y`. The type of the function is `Int => Boolean`.

  There is yet another function, `higher`, that takes a function as a parameter and returns a function.

- The type of `higher` is `(Int => Boolean) => (Int => Boolean)`.

- Let's break it down for better understanding. We can look at the type as `f1 => f2`.

  Here, both `f1` and `f2` are functions.

- The type of the `f1` function is `Int => Boolean`. The function takes an `Int` parameter and returns a `Boolean` value. The type of the function `f2` is the same: `Int => Boolean`. These points are pictorially represented in the following diagram:

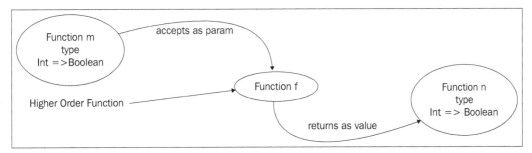

Figure 6.1:Disecting a higher order function

By the way, a function taking another as a parameter is a higher order function. The function **f** is a higher order function.

Let's look closely at a simple function:

```scala
scala> val f = (s: String) => s + s
f: String => String = <function1>
```

Here, the function `f` is taking in a `String` object as a parameter. What is a Scala function really? A Scala function is just an object, implementing one of the function traits. A function trait has an abstract `apply` method, which the object implements as shown in this code:

```scala
scala> val f : (String) => String = new Function1[String,
    |    String] {
```

```
    |     override def apply(s: String): String = s + s
    | }
f: String => String = <function1>
```

You can write n as shown in the following code:

```
scala> val n = new Function1[Int, Boolean] {
    |     def apply(y: Int): Boolean = y < 11
    | }
n: Int => Boolean = <function1>


scala> n(10)
res1: Boolean = true


scala> n(12)
res2: Boolean = false
```

Voila! We hit another Scala sweet spot! Instead of this long and wordy version, Scala sugars the pill and you can get away with just the following command:

```
val n = (y: Int) => y < 11
```

Roping in a scope

A variable lives in a scope. A scope defines an area, for example, the body of a function where variables exist. A **lexical scope** (also known as **static scope**) defines how variable names are resolved in nested functions. Inner functions contain the scope of enclosing (parent) functions.

Variables defined in the parent functions are available to the inner functions. Variables have the habit of coming in and going out of a scope.

For example, consider the following Java code snippet:

```
...
int v = 9;
...
for (int v = 0; v < 10; ++v) { // compilation error
    // Do something
}
```

The compiler will flag an error, as there is already another variable v in the scope.

Why does the following, slightly weird, Java code compile though? Let's check:

```
int k = 0;
{
    int i = 1; // 1
    k += i;
}
{
    int i = 1; // 2
    k += i;
}
System.out.println(k);
```

It compiles fine because blocks introduce a scope. Both the variables, on 1 and 2, are different although they are both named `i`. When a new block starts, a new scope starts. When the block ends, the scope ends, and all variables living in that scope cease to exist. Refer to the following figure for an example of scope:

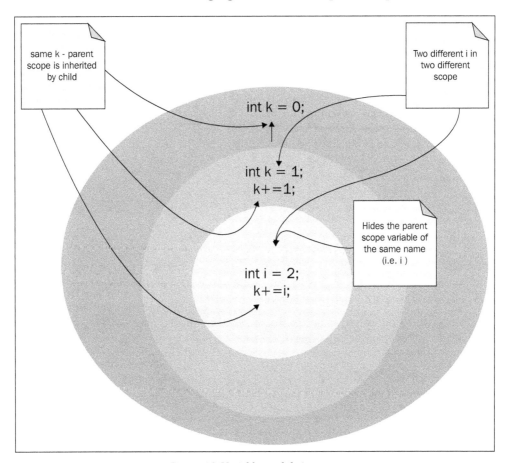

Figure 6.2: Variables and their scopes

Note that **k** is accessible as it is in an **enclosing scope**. A variable not defined in the current scope is a **free variable**. A free variable needs to be found and bound eventually. Consider the following code snippet as an example:

```
public interface SomeInterface {
  public void printMsg();
}
...
private SomeInterface create (final int k) {
    SomeInterface p = new SomeInterface() {

      @Override
      public void printMsg() {
        System.out.println(k); // 1
      }

    };
    return p;
  }
...
// Driver code
public static void main(String[] args) {
    Driver c = new Driver();
SomeInterface c1 = c.create(10); // 2
    SomeInterface c2 = c.create(20); // 3

 c1.printMsg(); // prints 10
c2.printMsg(); // prints 20
  }
```

The salient points for the preceding code are as follows:

- Note that the variable k is defined in an enclosing scope. It is a method parameter, that is, k exists in the method scope. The method scope **encloses** the variable p and the printMsg() method body.

- The variable k remains accessible even after the someMethod() method ends. Even if the variable falls out of scope because the method ended, it is alive and accessible.

- We return an instance of SomeInterface. The instance is stored in c1. When we invoke the printMsg() method, it prints 10, as k is bound to 10.

- The c2 closure is another SomeInterface instance. It prints 20, as k is bound to 20.

A best practice is to declare **a variable at first use**. Following this practice makes the code more readable. The following declaration is a bad style:

```
int j = 0;
int k = 0;
for(; j < 10; ++j)
```

For more information on declaring the variable at first, refer to `http://c2.com/cgi/wiki?DeclareVariablesAtFirstUse`.

There is a related refactoring too (Replace Assignment With Initialization), which you can find at:

```
http://www.refactoring.com/catalog/
replaceAssignmentWithInitialization.html
```

In Eclipse, this refactoring is available as the `Join` variable declaration.

Local functions – hiding and biding their time

Java classes have private methods. These private methods hide implementation details. Scala supports this way of hiding but also allows us to nest functions by making it easy to create local functions. We have already seen an example earlier when we looked at recursion. Our `count` function hid implementation details by nesting the work horse function:

```
def count(list: List[Int]): Int = { // the facade
  @tailrec
  def countIt(l: List[Int], acc: Int): Int = 1 match { // The work
horse
  // omitting body...
  }
  countIt(list, 0) // call the real thing
}
```

As good kids, we should hide the innards of how we really implemented the counting. The caller is not really interested in whether we are using tail recursion and the accumulator idiom.

The local function has a scope of its own. Let's try the following commands:

```
scala> def f(n: Int) = {
     |    val k = (y: Int) => y < n // 1
     |    k
```

```
  | }
f: (n: Int) Int => Boolean

scala> val p = f(10)   // n is 10 // 2
p: Int => Boolean = <function1>

scala> p(4)
res0: Boolean = true

scala> p(11)
res1: Boolean = false
```

The salient points for the preceding code are as follows:

- We have the val, k, which is a function. It takes an Int parameter, y, and compares it with n. If y is lower than n it returns true, otherwise false.

- We pass in the value 10. The result is a predicate function. A predicate is a function that returns a Boolean value. This predicate function accepts an integer argument and compares it with 10.

Now, let's try the following commands to make use of a filter method:

```
scala> def between(n: Int, m: Int) = {
  |     val k = (y: Int) => y >= n && y <= m // 1
  |     k
  | }
between: (n: Int, m: Int) Int => Boolean

scala> val nums: List[Int] = List(10, 20, 30, 40, 50)
nums: List[Int] = List(10, 20, 30, 40, 50)

scala> nums filter(between(20, 40))
res2: List[Int] = List(20, 30, 40)

scala> nums filter(between(1, 100))
res3: List[Int] = List(10, 20, 30, 40, 50)

scala> nums partition(between(20,40))
res4: (List[Int], List[Int]) = (List(20, 30, 40),List(10, 50))
```

We very much want to use the collection `filter` method. However, in this case, as it is applied to `nums`, filter expects a function that takes a number and returns a Boolean.

Local functions have their own scope. A simple thing to remember is whenever we use the curly braces { }, we are creating a scope. Though we don't use any braces while defining the local function, the scope is still there. The variables, n and m, are free variables in the local function. These are bound to the variables that are in an enclosing scope.

Here is how the pictorial representation looks:

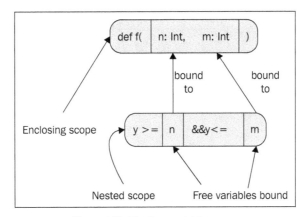

Figure 6.03: The free variables scope

The underscore – Scala's Swiss army knife

The underscore is an amazing thing that comes in handy in many situations. Here are some uses of the underscore that we need to know about. We will deal with other exotic uses as we come across them.

A Scala method is a part of a class. A method has a name and a signature. You can also put annotations in a method. We have already seen the `@tailrec` annotation in *Chapter 3, Recursion and Chasing Your Own Tail*.

On the other hand, a function in Scala is an object or, moreover, an object implementing one of the function traits. A one parameter function implements Function1, a two parameter function implements Function 2 and so on.

When we create a variable whose value is a function object and when we call this function, the call gets converted into a call to the apply method.

Methods in Scala are not values, but functions in Scala are values. And as we know, we can pass these around. A method can also be converted to a function through **Eta expansion**, which is the fancy term used for this conversion. Let's type the following commands, for example, to try out this conversion:

```
scala> def m() = 3
m: () Int
scala> val k = m // m is invoked
k: Int = 3
```

When we just mention m, the method is invoked. Now, let's see how to assign the function itself. One way to do this is to specify an explicit type annotation as shown in this code:

```
scala> val k: () => Int = m
k: () => Int = <function0>
```

The other way is to apply the underscore with the method, as shown here:

```
scala> val k = m _
k: () => Int = <function0>
scala> k()
res2: Int = 3
```

This is also known as **lifting** a method into a function. Here is a method that multiplies its argument by 2 and returns the result:

```
scala> def mult(n: Int) = n * 2
mult: (n: Int) Int


scala> val mult_fun = mult _
mult_fun: Int => Int = <function1>
```

This is the Eta expansion that is used to lift a method:

```
scala> mult_fun(9)
res8: Int = 18
```

The conversion is as if we have written the following:

```
scala> val exp_multi_fun = new Function[Int, Int]  {
     |    override def apply(n: Int): Int = mult(n)
     | }
exp_multi_fun: Function[Int,Int] = <function1>
```

```
scala> exp_multi_fun(9)
res9: Int = 18
```

Anonymous functions use the underscore as an unnamed parameter for brevity. For example:

```
scala> List(1, 2, 3, 4) map { x => x * 2 }
res2: List[Int] = List(2, 4, 6, 8)
```

We can just type the following command with anonymous function:

```
scala> List(1, 2, 3, 4) map { _ * 2 }
res6: List[Int] = List(2, 4, 6, 8)
```

The underscore, _, acts as a placeholder for parameters. Each time an underscore is used, it refers to a different parameter:

```
scala> val sum = List(1,2,3).reduceLeft((a,b) => a + b)
sum: Int = 6
can be expressed more concisely as
scala> val sum = List(1,2,3).reduceLeft(_+_)
sum: Int = 6
```

The underscore is also used to match and throw away the uninteresting parts. For example, to pick up the first two elements of a tuple:

```
scala> val (x, y, _, _) = (7, 3, 9, 15)
x: Int = 7
y: Int = 3
```

The first two elements are taken from the right-hand side list and assigned to x and y. The third and fourth elements are ignored through the use of the _ element.

When we specify one or more arguments to a function and leave one or more arguments unspecified, we get another function. More specifically, we get a partially applied function, for example:

```
scala> def modBy(n: Int, d: Int) = n % d
modBy: (n: Int, d: Int)Int
```

We've seen nothing surprising so far. Just a method taking two parameters, n and d and computing the modulus of n divided by d.

Check out the following example where modBy is assigned to the funModBy function:

```
scala> val funMobBy = modBy _
funMobBy: (Int, Int) => Int = <function2>
```

Let's fix the value of d, at 2, thereby converting a two-argument function into a one-argument function. Can you see the <function1>? This modBy2 function is a **partially applied function**:

```
scala> val modBy2 = modBy(_: Int, 2)
modBy2: Int => Int = <function1>
```

It is as if we have written something like this command:

```
scala> val modBy2 = (n:Int) => n % 2
modBy2: Int => Int = <function1>
```

Instead of 2, if we now pass 3, we get another partially applied function:

```
scala> val modBy3 = modBy(_: Int, 3)
modBy3: Int => Int = <function1>
```

So now, we fix d at 3. Using the underscore, we can leave the parameter open. Now, you can pass in any integer number as the first argument.

Using _ in place of a parameter, we have converted a two-argument function into a one-argument function. In other words, we specified the argument list **partially**. Hence, the functions modBy2 and modBy3 are **partially defined**.

Does this sound familiar? Remember we discussed factories in from *Chapter 2, Singletons, Factories, and Builders*? Yes, the mechanism looks a lot like a factory. The underscore really scores!

A taste of the curry

There is another way we can write the method, where each parameter is enclosed in parenthesis. For example, the modBy2 method can also be written as follows:

```
scala> def modBy2(n: Int)(d: Int) = n % d
modBy2: (n: Int)(d: Int)Int

scala> modBy2(10)(3)
res0: Int = 1
```

This form is called **currying**. Currying allows us to turn a function that expects two arguments into a function that expects only one.

By applying currying to modBy2, we get back another function:

```
scala> modBy2 _
res3: Int => (Int => Int) = <function1>
```

This is a function that takes in an Int parameter, n. It returns another function, which takes yet another Int parameter, d. This function finally returns the result, which is Int. Well, here is the diagrammatic representation of currying:

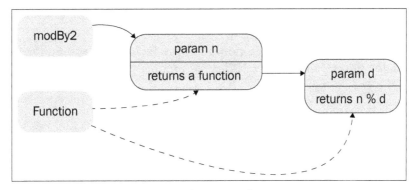

Figure 6.4: The currying function

If we just specify the value for n, we get a partially applied function again:

```
scala> modBy2(10) _
res5: Int => Int = <function1>


scala> val p = modBy2(10) _  // n is fixed to 10
p: Int => Int = <function1>


scala> p(2)
res6: Int = 0   // 10 % 2


scala> p(3) // 10 % 3
res7: Int = 1
```

You can convert a method to a curried form as shown in this code snippet:

```
scala> def m(m: Int, n: Int, o: Int, p: String) = s"${m % n + o}" + p
m: (m: Int, n: Int, o: Int, p: String)String


scala> val p = (m _).curried
```

```
p: Int => (Int => (Int => (String => String))) = <function1>

scala> p(10)(4)(2)("th")
res9: String = 4th
```

Here are some examples, where the currying form is a clear winner.

Type inference

The following snippet shows a method, firstMatching, that takes a List of the type T elements and a predicate function. This is a generic method that returns [T], which holds the first element that satisfies the predicate. If there is no such element, it returns None:

```
object NoTypeInference extends App {
  def firstMatching[T](xs: List[T], f: (T) => Boolean): Option[T] = xs
match {
    case Nil => None
    case x :: ts => if (f(x)) Some(x) else firstMatching(ts, f)
  }

  println(firstMatching(List(1,2,3,4), (x: Int) => x < 2))   // Some(1)
  println(firstMatching(List("hi", "hello", "some", "one"), (x:String)
=> x.length >= 5)) // Some(hello)
}
```

We need to pass the function, specifying the parameter type, Int, or string for x:

```
object CurriedTypeInference extends App {
  def firstMatching[T](xs: List[T])(f: (T) => Boolean): Option[T] = xs
match {
    case Nil => None
    case x :: ts => if (f(x)) Some(x) else firstMatching(ts)(f)
  }

  println(firstMatching(List(1, 2, 3, 4))(_ < 2))
  println(firstMatching(List("hi", "hello", "some", "one"))(_.length
>= 5))
}
```

When we use the curried form, the compiler infers (figures out) the type, T, which is an Int. We can even elide the name of the parameter, x, and have a short, succinct, and sweet definition of the predicate function.

Of implicits and explicits

We are soon going to talk a lot about moms and their kids. Here is a small example of a case where currying comes in useful:

```scala
scala> implicit def housewife = "Housewife"
housewife: String


scala> def f(momName: String)(implicit worksAs: String) =
     |    println(s"Mom ${momName} works as ${worksAs}")
f: (momName: String)(implicit worksAs: String)Unit


scala> f("Sheela")
Mom Sheela works as Housewife


scala> f("Nisha")("Software Engineer")
Mom Nisha works as Software Engineer
```

Scala supports marking parameters as implicit. However, we don't want the momName implicit. The following simply does not work!

```scala
scala> implicit val housewife = "Housewife"
housewife: String = Housewife


scala> def f(implicit momName: String, worksAs: String) =
     |    println(s"Mom ${momName} works as ${worksAs}")
f: (implicit momName: String, implicit worksAs: String)Unit


scala> f
Mom Housewife works as Housewife // OOPS!
```

Both the parameters got marked for an implicit resolution.

Stylish blocks

Style matters! Easy-to-read code is always sporty, looks nicer, and is easier to grok. Here is a method that takes two parameters: an integer and a predicate function. The method calls the predicate with the integer parameter as an argument:

```scala
scala> def matches(n: Int)(f: (Int) => Boolean) = {
     |    if(f(n))
```

```
|         println("Matches")
|     else
|         println("Nope")
| }
matches: (n: Int)(f: Int => Boolean)Unit
scala> matches(4)(_ == 4) // 1
Matches
scala> matches(4) { x =>   // 2
|         x == 4
| }
Matches
scala> matches(4) { _ == 4 } // works too
Matches
```

The cases marked as 1 and 2 are the same. Scala usually allows braces instead of parentheses, and in this case, they perk the code up.

The loan pattern

C++ programmers chant a mantra — **Resource Acquisition Is Initialization (RAII)**. The constructor of an object acquires a finite resource (for example, files, heap memory, db connection, mutex locks), and the destructor, frees them.

RAII is a resource-management technique. No matter how a control flow returns, a control flow returns the destructor that is guaranteed to be invoked. A method/function could exit its scope via an earlier return or due to an exception thrown.

In C++, an object's lifetime is bound by its scope. When a scope is entered, the object is created, that is, its constructor is invoked. In the constructor invocation, we acquire the resource. When the scope is finally exited either via an early return or due to an exception, the object destructor is invoked. In the destructor code, we can release the resource.

For more information on RAII, refer to https://www.hackcraft.net/raii/.

One famous use of this technique is the auto_ptr template and its friends, such as shared_ptr. For more on this, refer to http://en.cppreference.com/w/cpp/memory/auto_ptr.

If we look at the pattern closely, we can see two parts—a common part and a variable part, which is unspecified and left blank that would be filled as the situation demands. The common part is a **boilerplate**. The variable part is, well, unspecified.

Scala is super good at eliminating the boilerplate. But what about the variable part? You guessed it right, the variable part is a function!

Take a look at the following example. Here, we read lines from a text file, reverse each line, and print it back on the console:

```
object ReadAFile extends App {
  import scala.io.Source
  val bufferedSource = Source.fromFile("example.txt")
  for (line <- bufferedSource.getLines) {
    println(line.reverse)
  }
  bufferedSource.close() // 1
}
```

We are using Scala's source to read a text file. The problem is at 1. Someone could forget to add these cleanup statements on some **possible exit** path from the method.

The loan pattern ensures that resources are cleaned up fine, now matter how we exit the code. The resource is just borrowed and used. Here is the pattern in action:

```
import scala.io.Source

object AutoCleanup extends App {

  def autoCleanUp[T](f: Source)(handler: Source => T): T = {
    try { // 1
      handler(f) // 2
    } finally {
      println("Closing resource")
      f.close()
    }
  }

  val s1 = Source.fromFile("/home/atul/myScala/example.txt")
  val s2 = Source.fromFile("/home/atul/myScala/example.txt")

  autoCleanUp(s1) { h =>
    for (line <- h.getLines) { // 3
      println(line.reverse)
```

```
        }
    }

    autoCleanUp(s2) { h =>
        for (line <- h.getLines) { // 4
            println(line.toCharArray.length + ":" + line)
        }
    }
}
```

how the flow looks pictorially:

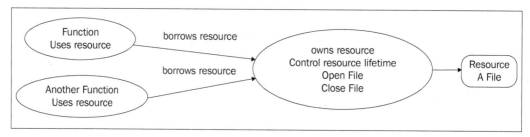

Figure 6.5: Borrowing resources -The loan pattern

This is pretty simple; the salient points of the preceding code are as follows:

- The `try/catch` method is the boilerplate. For any resource of the source type, this method takes on the mantle of releasing it after invoking the function.

- The `handler` function is called when we pass `f` as an argument.

- Now, we pass in a function that reads lines of a file, reverses each line, and prints it.

- Then, we pass in another function that reads lines of a file and prints each line that is prefixed with the length of the line.

Serving the curry

Duplicated code is a major code smell. We need to apply the extract method refactoring to remove this smell. For more information, refer to `https://sourcemaking.com/refactoring/extract-method`.

Instead of copying and pasting, we should reuse the code. One example of such code reuse is the template method design pattern. We have a common algorithm shell. This shell has blanks, that is, unspecified behavior. The blanks are filled with a specific behavior as needed. Too formal and pedantic? Let's come back to our real-world example and look at moms and their kids.

In our example, there are moms who have different professions. There are working moms, engineer moms, doctor moms, and teacher moms. All moms love their kids. This is the common part. However, an engineer mom will fix machines, design algorithms, and build houses. On the other hand, a doctor mom will perform surgeries, prescribe medicines to the patients, and take care of newborn babies. A teacher mom will teach children how to read and write. (And I am not even talking of professor moms!). A defense scientist mom won't want to talk about her work. At the end of the day, most moms love to cook for their kids and feed them. This is the common part. And all moms surely will talk nonstop about their kids. This again is the common part.

An algorithm to map out a mom's day will be a mix of this common part, and many additional specialized bits thrown in. Refer to the following diagram as an example of a template method that shows a mom's regular day:

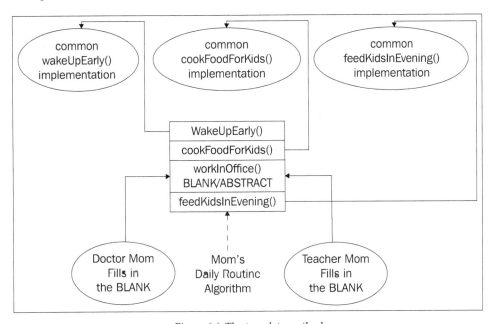

Figure 6.6: The template method

Here is the Java code for the preceding method:

```java
// Mom.java

package chapter06;

import java.util.List;

import com.google.common.base.Joiner;
import com.google.common.collect.Lists;

public abstract class Mom {

    protected abstract List<String> mumsOfficeTaskList(); // 1

    public String getHerDailyRoutine() {
    final List<String> commonMumTasks =
Lists.newArrayList(wakesUpEarly(),
        cooksFoodForKids(), feedKidsInEvening());
    final List<String> herOfficeTasks = mumsOfficeTaskList();

        return makeADailyRoutineMsg(commonMumTasks, herOfficeTasks);
    }

    private String makeADailyRoutineMsg(final List<String>
commonMumTasks,
    final List<String> herOfficeTasks) { // 2
    final List<String> allTasks = Lists
        .newArrayList("---Daily Routine For a mum---");
    allTasks.addAll(commonMumTasks);
    allTasks.addAll(formatOfficeRoutine(herOfficeTasks));
    allTasks.add("---Thats all a mum can do in a day!---");

        final String allTasksMsgList = Joiner.on("\n").join(allTasks);
        return allTasksMsgList;
    }

    private List<String> formatOfficeRoutine(final List<String> workMsg)
{
        final List<String> formattedMsgList = Lists
            .newArrayList("My office routine");
        for (final String msg : workMsg) {
        formattedMsgList.add("\t" + msg);
    }
    formattedMsgList.add("No more shop talk");
```

```
    return formattedMsgList;
    }

    private String feedKidsInEvening() {
    return "Feeding kids in the evening";
    }

  private String cooksFoodForKids() {
   return "Cooking Food for my kids";
  }

  private String wakesUpEarly() {
   return "Sprightly mum I am - waking up!!!";
  }


}
```

As you can see, the template method is an algorithmic shell. The salient points for the preceding code are as follows:

- This is the blank that a subclass needs to fill. Every mom's office tasks are different and depend on where she works. A doctor mom can tell us about her daily office chores, but a defense scientist mom would rather keep mum, if you may!
- This is the algorithm that takes the common tasks that each mom performs. It takes this **common part**, combines it with the specifics of her office chores (this part **varies**), formats it all nicely, and prints it.

The DoctorMom implementation is shown in the following code. Here, you can check out the source code for a running example:

```
import java.util.List;

import com.google.common.collect.Lists;

public class DoctorMom extends Mom {

 @Override
 protected final List<String> mumsOfficeTaskList() {
   final List<String> dailyOfficeTasks = Lists.newArrayList(
     "Get to the hospital", "Talk To Patients", "Perform
Sugeries");
   return dailyOfficeTasks;
 }


}
```

Note that a mom's office task list is an internal implementation detail. It is just overridable, but is not exposed to the outside world.

Here is how we can express a similar design in Scala:

```scala
object MomAndKids extends App {

  def feedKidsInEvening() = "Feeding kids in the evening"

  def cookFoodForKids() = "Cooking food for my kids"

  def wakeUpEarly() = "Sprightly mum I am - waking up!!!\""

  case class DoctorMom() {
    def herOfficeRoutine = List("Go to hospital", "See patients",
  "Perform surgeries") // variable part
  }

  case class DefenceScientistMom() {
    def herOfficeRoutine = List("This mum", "Will keep mum") // Need
  to maintain secrecy! Can't talk about it!
    // variable part
  }

  def makeADailyRoutineMsg(commonTasks: () => List[String])
  (officeTasks: () => List[String]) = { // 1
    // the 'template method' algorithm
    val herOfficeTasks = officeTasks() map { x => s"\t${x}" } // 2
    commonTasks() ::: List("My office routine") ::: herOfficeTasks :::
  List("No more shop talk")
  }

  def printDailyRoutine(msgList: List[String]) = {
    println("---Daily Routine For a mum---")
    msgList foreach (println(_))
    println("---Thats all a mum can do in a day!---")
  }

  def commonMumTasks = List(wakeUpEarly(), cookFoodForKids(),
  feedKidsInEvening())

  val mom1 = DoctorMom()
```

```
    printDailyRoutine(makeADailyRoutineMsg(commonMumTasks _)(mom1.
herOfficeRoutine _)) // 3

  val mom2 = DefenceScientistMom()
  printDailyRoutine(makeADailyRoutineMsg(commonMumTasks _)(mom2.
herOfficeRoutine _))


}
```

Here are the salient points of the preceding code:

- The `commonTasks` parameter is a function that takes no arguments and returns `List[String]`. Similarly, `officeTasks` is a parameter that is yet another function that takes no arguments and returns `List[String]`. Both these parameters have the same type.

- We invoke the `officeTasks` function, and prepend a tab to each result line. In the next line, we assemble all the parts. This is the template method wherein we piece together the common part and the variable part.

- Note the use of underscore again. It is converting methods into functions.

However, we still have some duplication. Note the use of the two calls shown here:

```
    printDailyRoutine(makeADailyRoutineMsg(commonMumTasks _)(mom1.
herOfficeRoutine _))
    printDailyRoutine(makeADailyRoutineMsg(commonMumTasks _)(mom2.
herOfficeRoutine _))
```

Yes, the highlighted part is a fixture, and the variable part is a function. Pretty quaint, isn't it? Not yet! We are specifying the common fixture twice! Here is an improved version:

```
    val commonTasks = makeADailyRoutineMsg(commonMumTasks _) _
// printDailyRoutine(makeADailyRoutineMsg(commonMumTasks _)(mom1.
herOfficeRoutine _))
  printDailyRoutine(commonTasks(mom1.herOfficeRoutine _))
  printDailyRoutine(commonTasks(mom2.herOfficeRoutine _))
```

The common algorithm, also known as the template method, is now held in `commonTasks`. The variable part, mom's office routine, is a function that is tacked on to realize the complete flow!

Frills and thrills – decorators again

In the last chapter, we looked at the decorator pattern and Scala's stackable modifications. Here is another way to use expression decorators. As we have had some curry, let's round it out with ice creams! Quite a feast there is today!

As if an ice cream itself is not enough a temptation, we have toppings as well. We will have nuts, jelly, and honey toppings. Feeling sinful already? Here comes the Scala version:

```scala
import scala.language.implicitConversions

object IceCreams extends App {
 sealed trait IceCreamType { // 1
  def price: Double
 }


 case object Vanilla extends IceCreamType { // 2
  val price = 10.0
 }
 case object Mango extends IceCreamType {
  val price = 20.0
 }

 implicit def iceCreamPriceWrapper(iceCreamType: IceCreamType): Double =
  iceCreamType.price // 3

 case class IceCream(price: Double) // 4

 def add(c: IceCream)(p: Double) =
  c.copy(price = c.price + p) // 5

 def addNuts(c: IceCream) = add(c)(15) // 6
 def addJelly(c: IceCream) = add(c)(25)
 def addHoney(c:IceCream) = add(c)(30)

 val withNuts = addNuts _ // 7
 val withJelly = addJelly _
```

```
val withHoney = addHoney _

val order1 = withJelly(withNuts(withHoney(IceCream(Vanilla))))
println(order1.price) // prints 80
val order2 = withJelly(withNuts(IceCream(Mango)))
println(order2.price) // prints 60
}
```

Pictorially, the example looks as shown in the following figure:

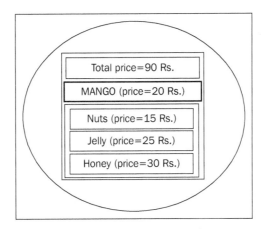

Figure 6.7: Decorating an ice cream with toppings

Here is how the code works:

- We have a `sealed trait` method that defines `iceCreamType`.

- There are two types of ice cream, `Vanilla` and `Mango`. You are right, these are enumerations. We also see how Scala allows us to override `def` with `val`.

- There is an implicit conversion from an ice cream type to `double`. Here, `double` is required, and as we pass in the ice cream type, the conversion kicks in. The price encoded in the type is used as the base price.

- A `case class` class takes the base price in its constructor.

- We have the price algorithm here. This is again the common part. It takes an ice cream, adds the topping price, and creates a new ice cream object. Note that the `price` attribute is immutable. As we have seen earlier, the copy idiom creates a copy of the `IceCream` object by just overriding the `price` attribute.

- Some toppings and their prices are expressed in terms of the common `add` algorithm. Note that the `add` algorithm is curried. The variable part is the topping's price. The nuts toppings are for Rs. 15 and the jelly toppings come at Rs. 25.

- We have partially applied functions for the toppings. Now, we leave the `IceCream` parameter open, as it is the variable part. However, we've fixed the topping price.

- Finally, we serve the ice creams. The the line `withJelly(withNuts(IceC ream(MANGO)))` decorates a base ice cream with toppings as specified. The toppings are decoupled from each other, just like in the Java implementation we saw earlier. Note also that you can mix toppings in any order!

This is a pretty sweet way to end the feast!

Wrapping it up

We need to add additional behavior to the existing code so as to address **cross-cutting** concerns. Logging is a cross-cutting concern, for example. We have an existing method whose arguments we need to log without modifying the method itself. Don't worry, we have currying to the rescue! Here is how the code looks:

```
object WrapItUp extends App {
  def attach_logger[X, Y](f: (X) => Y)(arg: X): Y = { // 1
    println("arg = " + arg.toString)
    println("Calling the function...")
    val result = f(arg)   // 2
    println("function call returned...")

    result
  }


  def f1(i: Integer): Integer = i + 10 // 3
  def f2(s: String): String = s + " " + s // 4


  val f1WithArgsLogged = attach_logger(f1) _ // 5 - attach argument
loggin
  val f2WithArgsLogged = attach_logger(f2) _ // without touching the
function


  println(s"Evaluating just f1 itself = ${f1(2)}\n")
  println(s"Evaluating f1 with logging = ${f1WithArgsLogged(2)}\n") // 6
```

```
    println(s"Evaluating just f2 itself = ${f2("hello")}\n")
    println(s"Evaluating f2 with logging ${f2WithArgsLogged("hello")}\n")
}
```

The salient points for the preceding code are as follows:

- Here, we have a curried method that takes two parameters. The first is a generic function itself, taking a single argument of the type X. This function returns a result of the type Y. The second parameter is an argument of the type X.

- Then, the logging statements are added. In real life, we would use a logging library such as Logback or Log4J. To keep it simple, we use the println statement.

- The actual method whose arguments we wish to log. This method takes an Integer and returns an Integer.

- Another method that takes String and returns String. The arguments of this method will be logged too.

- Then, we attach the logger to the function. The f1WithArgsLogged and f2WithArgsLogged functions are partially defined. The function itself is the common part, and the actual argument is a variable.

- After this, the method itself is called. Next, we call the method with the logging attached.

Summary

In this chapter, you learned about functions. We talked about Scala functions that are first-class values. This means that we can pass them as arguments and return them as values. You learned about variable scopes and bindings and an important concept called closure. We looked at some amazing uses for the underscore, which is termed as Scala's Swiss army knife. Armed with the know-how of local functions, closures, and scope, we looked at partially applied functions and currying. We also saw how currying and partially applied forms are compared with each other.

These are very useful techniques as illustrated by the loan pattern. This is a resource lifecycle pattern similar to the RAII idiom in C++. Next, we looked at the template method design pattern, its applicability, and the Java version. The Scala version is short and sweet, thanks to the partially applied functions.

In the last chapter, we looked at the decorator design pattern, and how Scala's stackable modifications help us achieve the same effect. Decorators can also be expressed using partially applied functions, as we saw in the ice cream example.

Finally, we had a taste of the aspects philosophy and how to add a behavior without touching the underlying method.

With all this know-how under the belt, let's look at the visitor pattern next. This is the recurring theme of the open/closed principle. We will see how pattern matching helps us implement visitor and other related idioms. Off we go!

7
Of Visitors and Chains of Responsibilities

In this chapter, we will look at two important design patterns, namely **visitors** and **chains of responsibilities**. These patterns help us model real-world scenarios in a pretty neat fashion. Let's first look at the problem domain.

Rakesh and Nita are happily married. One fine evening, Rakesh gets pleasantly surprised as Prakash comes visiting. Prakash is his childhood buddy and is in town on business. Prakash gets to know of Rakesh living in the same town and comes home, and the buddies meet after a span of many years. Prakash is meeting his friend's wife for the first time, though. They greet each other, well, a little formally. Prakash and Rakesh, on the other hand, back slap each other and enquire about each other's family and have a lot of memories to reminisce about.

We can imagine a similar situation ensuing when Nita's schoolmates come visiting the couple. Rakesh and Nita's mates would greet each other a little formally. The behavior depends on who is greeting whom. We could model Rakesh and Nita as subclasses of FamilyMembers (Husband and Wife) and their mates as Friends. Using the FamilyMember and Friend abstractions, we need to write code so that the correct greetings are exchanged. We will see how the visitor design pattern helps here.

The other problem we will look at is how to handle responsibilities. An employee alone cannot cope with all the work at an office, for example. Workplaces have intuitively built the chains of responsibilities so that a task is passed on to the employee who has the necessary skills.

This division of labor is the underlying theme for the chain of responsibility pattern. Software systems, too, use the division of labor pattern to create processing pipelines. This pipelining is a very powerful construct that promotes reuse and allows us to spend time assembling the processing instead of rebuilding everything from scratch.

We will see how we can build processing pipe lines with Scala functions. However, we will need some know-how of related techniques, namely, pattern matching and partial functions. We will take a detour through them, trying out examples in the REPL, to get a good footing.

The chain of responsibilities Java implementation will let us appreciate the benefits of chaining objects together. We will see how partial functions help us realize the chain of responsibilities in Scala. You will also learn about the collect idiom in the context of partial functions. Let's get going!

A tale of two hierarchies

Let's look at two class hierarchies, a family member and its friends. A family member's hierarchy is kind of fixed over time. It includes a husband, wife, and kids. However, friends get added at some point of time in their life. A wife may suddenly meet her college friend after many years, or a husband comes across his childhood buddy after a span of many years. Let's have a look at the pictorial representation of this:

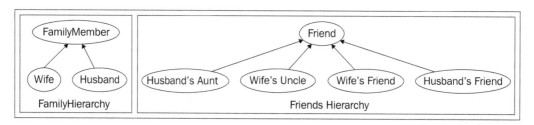

Figure 7.1: The two hierarchies

The question is how do we know who is greeting whom, for example, a friend of the husband will be somewhat formal in greeting the wife. On the other hand, the same friend can go back slapping the husband, as they are old buddies. To resolve this, we need to know both the concrete instances of `FamilyMember` and `Friend`. Here is a first cut, using `instanceof`:

```
if (friend instanceof HusbandsFriend && familyMember
  instanceof Wife) {
  System.out.println("How do you do, Mr. " +
    friend.getName());
}
else if (friend instanceof HusbandsFriend && familyMember
  instanceof Husband) {
  System.out.println("Hey budd, " + friend.getName() + ", how is
life old man!!!");
}-.
```

Testing for concrete object types, using the instanceof operator, is a **code smell**. When we plan to support `WifesFriend`, we need to remember changing this code to accommodate the new friend. In a big system, there might be many such places. If we forget to add the requisite clauses even in one place, we have a broken system.

How could we better this? Instead of asking an object about its state or type and then performing actions based on this, we tell the object to do something and let the object decide how to do it. This is the the **Tell-Don't-Ask** principle.

In this way, if the object changes the algorithm, the changes need to happen in one place, that is, in the class method(s).

The design should also allow us to add newer types of friends, that is, subclasses of `Friend`. In our case, we wish to stay away from hunting down the base class references.

In other words, for the preceding code based on `instanceof`, we should perform the **Replace conditional with polymorphism** refactoring.

Instead of testing for object types, we should use polymorphism. For this, we simply need to put the conditional behavior in the subclass method.

> For more information on the same, you can refer to the following links:
>
> * `http://www.javapractices.com/topic/`
>   `TopicAction.do?Id=31`
>
> and
>
> `https://sourcemaking.com/refactoring/replace-`
> `conditional-with-polymorphism`

One alternative design is to add an overloaded method for each concrete subclass of `Friend`:

```
public abstract class FamilyMember {
  public abstract void greet(HusbandsFriend husbandsFriend);
  public abstract void greet(WifesFriend wifesFriend);
  ...
public class Husband extends FamilyMember {
  @Override
  public void greet(HusbandsFriend husbandsFriend) {
    ...
  }
```

```
    @Override
    public void greet( WifesFriend wifesFriend) {
       ...
    }
}
```

Now, at any point, when we have **a new type of friend**, the `FamilyMember` class needs to be change.

Instead of this, could we send a polymorphic dispatch to both `FamilyMember` and its `Friend`? The greetings depend on their dynamic types. However, how can we get a dispatch on two references? The language provided dynamic dispatch works on a single reference only. When we need a dynamic dispatch on two references, we need a way to simulate double dispatch, such as using the visitor pattern.

The Visitor pattern

We have a **FamilyMember** hierarchy, as shown in the following figure, which is pretty stable. We have another hierarchy, `Friends`, which is pretty open ended. So now, a **FamilyMember** needs to accept a **Friend**.

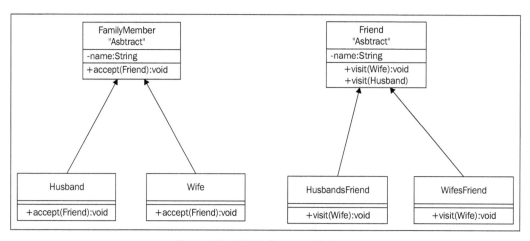

Figure 7.2: A UML diagram — Visitors

When we have a hierarchy and we need to add a new method to it **without** modifying it, we use the **visitor pattern**. Here is the code snippet for this example:

```
public abstract class FamilyMember {

  .
  private String name;

  public FamilyMember(String name) {
    this.name = name;
  }

  public String getName() {
    return name;
  }

  public abstract void accept(Friend friend); // 1
}

public class Husband extends FamilyMember {

  public Husband(String name) {
    super(name);
  }

  @Override
  public void accept(Friend friend) { // 2
    friend.greet(this); // 3
  }

}
```

The salient points of the preceding example are as follows:

- Here, we have an `accept` method, accepting all friends. The `FamilyMember` hierarchy opens up its doors for `Friends` to visit.
- The visit takes place—the `Friend` object is `greetedBy` the `FamilyMember` concrete instance. I am showing only the abstraction, `Friend`, and the concrete `HusbandsFriend` class. For the complete example, refer to the book's source code.

The `Friend` hierarchy looks as the following snippet:

```
public abstract class Friend { // 1
private String name;

public Friend(String name) {
  this.name = name;
}

public String getName() {
  return name;
}

public abstract void greet(Husband husband); // 2

public abstract void greet(Wife wife); // 3
}

public class HusbandsFriend extends Friend {

public HusbandsFriend(String name) {
  super(name);
}

@Override
public void greet(Husband husband) { // 4
  System.out.println("Hey budd, " + husband.getName() + ", how
    is life old man!!!"); // and lots of
 // back slapping etc. etc.
}

@Override
public void greet(Wife wife) { // 5
System.out.println("How do you do, Mrs. " + wife.getName());
}

}
```

The salient points of the preceding example are as follows:

- The `Friend` hierarchy is a root class
- The abstraction where the friend greets `Husband` — note the concrete parameter type, `Husband`, is concrete
- A friend greets `Wife` — again, the parameter is concrete

- Friend and husband meet—by this time, we have figured out **both**, `Friend` and `FamilyMember` (`Husband`)

- Friend greets wife. We know now both `Friend` and `FamilyMember` (`Wife`)

The crux of this is the first dispatch in the `accept` call. This call **resolves** `FamilyMember`. Even though we don't know the type at compile time, the method of the concrete runtime object is called.

We know the **static type** of the `FamilyMember` class when we are executing in the `accept` method. When we call `greet`, the **dynamic dispatch** again kicks in! After this, we land into a concrete `overloaded Friend.greet(...)` method. Here is a diagram to understand this better:

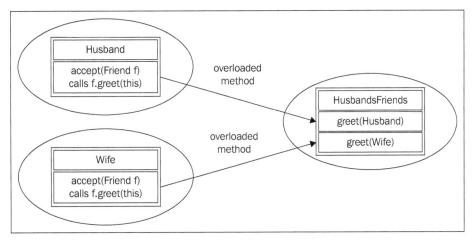

Figure 7.3: The double dispatch

Many hues of pattern matching

Before we get into the Scalaish way of doing double dispatching, we need to know and appreciate Scala's pattern matching. Pattern matching is Scala's Swiss army knife feature, as it is that handy! We can use it instead of conditional statements. Pattern matching is also used to destructure an object. We have already seen how a list is destructured into its head and tail in *Chapter 3, Tail Recursion – and Chasing Your Own Tail*. Instead of type casting, you can pattern match on the type of an object. Pattern matches can be used with these objects. Code using tuples can be made pleasantly readable with the help of pattern matches. We will see all these usages by playing with small code snippets in the REPL.

Case classes are blessed with convenient methods, making them amenable to pattern matching. Also, there is a deep connection between pattern matching and partial functions as we will soon see. So, let's get our hands dirty by running to the REPL.

Just like if/else, pattern matching matches any sort of data, and the first match is returned as shown here:

```scala
scala> val k = 1
k: Int = 1

scala>

scala> k match {
     |    case 1 => "One"
     |    case 2 => "Two"
     |    case _ => "Anything other than One or Two"
     | }

String = One
```

The third pattern is a wildcard pattern. It is a catch-all pattern. What happens if we omit it? Try it. Just omit the wildcard pattern match and assign 3 to k. You will get a MatchError error.

The match also takes into account the type, for example:

```scala
scala> def stringify(k: Any): String = {
     |    k match {
     |      case 1 => "One"
     |      case "One" => "1"
     |      case _ => "Not a one"
     |    }
     | }
stringify: (k: Any)String

scala>

scala> stringify(1)
res3: String = One
scala> printIt("One")
res4: String = 1
```

De-structuring

We have already seen the destructuring feature for lists. The `cons operator (::)` is used both to create a list and to destructure it. Destructuring a list refer to separating the head (the first element) of the list and the tail (the remaining elements), as shown here:

```scala
scala> val list = 1 :: 2 :: 3 :: Nil // cons operator constructs the list
list: List[Int] = List(1, 2, 3)


scala>


scala> list match {
     |     case x :: xs => println("Head = " + x) //cons operator for de-
structuring
     |    // case _ => println("Headless!")
     | }
<console>:12: warning: match may not be exhaustive.
It would fail on the following input: Nil
       list match {
       ^

Head = 1
```

The nice part here is the warning. We get it at the compilation time instead of the unwelcome message at runtime. Earlier, it was mentioned that the `case` classes are amenable to pattern matching. Here is an example of restructuring an object:

```scala
scala> abstract class Parent
defined class Parent


scala> case class Mom(worksAs: String) extends Parent
defined class Mom


scala> case class Dad(worksAs: String) extends Parent
defined class Dad


scala> def tellUsAboutYourParents(p: Parent) =
     |    p match {
     |       case Dad(worksAs) => println(s"Dad is a ${worksAs}") // 1
```

```
    |      case Mom(worksAs) => println(s"Mom is a ${worksAs}")
    |      case _ => println("???")
    |   }
tellUsAboutYourParents: (p: Parent)Unit


scala> tellUsAboutYourParents(Dad("Lawyer"))
Dad is a Lawyer
```

At the part of code labeled as 1, the case expression destructures the object. After this, we can reach into the innards of the Dad object and access the worksAs attribute.

Typed patterns

We can reach at the runtime type of an object with the help of pattern matching. In the following snippet, we match on the runtime, concrete type of the parameter, p:

```
scala> def typeMe(p: Any) = p match {
    |      case s: String => println(s.reverse)
    |      case i: Int => println(i*i)
    |      case _ => println("???")
    | }
typeMe: (p: Any)Unit


scala> typeMe("Hi")
iH


scala> typeMe(23)
529


scala> typeMe(23.32)
???
```

We will be using this feature to code our double dispatch (in the next section).

Pattern guards

If we put an if condition after the pattern, the condition becomes a **pattern guard**.
Here an example of pattern guards

```
scala> val k = 1
k: Int = 1

scala>

scala> k match {
     |    case i: Int if i   >= 1 && i <= 9 => println("Within Range")
     |    case _ => println("Huh?")
     | } Within Range
```

The first clause is only matched if the condition is met; otherwise, the wildcard
takes over.

Tuple explosion

You can de-structure a tuple with pattern matching. This allows us to bind variables
to the tuple's members:

```
scala> def explodeTuple(t: (Int, Int, Int)) = t match {
     |    case (x, y, z) => println(s"x = ${x}, y = ${y}, z = ${z}")
     | }
explodeTuple: (t: (Int, Int, Int))Unit

scala>

scala> explodeTuple((1,2,3))
x = 1, y = 2, z = 3
```

This helps us to avoid the t._1, t._2 syntax and makes the code a little readable.

You can also use patterns to define multiple variables at the same time, as shown
here:

```
scala> val (n, s) = (1, "hi")
n: Int = 1
s: String = hi
```

Here is an interesting case where we have a case class and a tuple:

```
scala> case class C(x: Int, y: String)
defined class C
scala> val c1 = C(2, "two")
c1: C = C(2,two)
```

This is the usual apply method that is invoked to construct the object:

```
scala> val C(p, q) = c1
p: Int = 2
q: String = two
```

Picking up only one member works too, as shown in the following code:

```
scala> val C(p, _) = c1
p: Int = 2
scala> val C(_, q) = c1
q: String = two
```

Now, here is a very interesting case of the nested list:

```
scala> case class C(x: Int, y: List[List[Int]])
defined class C
```

The y nested list is a list within a list that has the unapply method:

```
scala> val c1 = C(1, List(List(11,22,33,44)))
c1: C = C(1,List(List(11, 22, 33, 44)))
scala> val (_, (_ :: q :: _) :: _) = C.unapply(c1).get
q: Int = 22
```

A case class has an unapply method. This method returns Option with Tuple inside.

Now we will pick up the second element (Int) of the first list.

Partial functions

In the previous chapter, we looked at partially applied functions. We left one or more arguments unspecified, and as a result, we got another function. There are partially applied functions and there are **partial functions**. So, what do we mean by the term partial functions? It simply means that such a function is not defined for some values. Let's try the following example of a partial function:

```scala
scala> val f = (x: Int, y: Int) => x / y
f: (Int, Int) => Int = <function2>


scala> f(12, 3)
res0: Int = 4


scala> f(12, 0)
java.lang.ArithmeticException: / by zero
  at $anonfun$1.apply$mcIII$sp(<console>:10)
  ... 33 elided
```

Here, we have a function that takes two integer parameters, x and y. It divides x by y. When we pass 0 as the value of y, we get a division by 0. The function f is not defined for a subset of possible values. Or rather, as it is partially defined for some values, it is a **partially defined function**. It is defined only for some values. Scala allows us to express a partial function as shown in the following code snippet:

```scala
scala> val f: PartialFunction[(Int, Int), Int] = {
     |    case (i, j) if  j != 0 => i / j
     | }
f: PartialFunction[(Int, Int),Int] = <function1>


scala> f.isDefinedAt(10, 0) // 1
res5: Boolean = false


scala> f.isDefinedAt(10, 10)
res6: Boolean = true
```

Note the partial function syntax in the preceding code. Here, we can check whether the function is defined for some input values.

The following pattern match is also partially defined:

```
val list = List(1,2,3)
list match {
  case x::xs => println("Head of the list " + x)
}
```

This pattern match does not take into account the case when a list will be empty! If the list is empty, then you will get a match error.

`List[A]` is also `PartialFunction[Int, A]` that maps indices to elements. The access is partially defined, only for indices which are within bounds.

```
scala> val list = List(1, 2, 3)
list: List[Int] = List(1, 2, 3)
```

If we try accessing the 99th element, we get an `IndexOutOfBoundsException` error.

Here is an interesting idiom illustrating how partial functions come handy!

In this example, we have a list of pairs where each pair holds an employee's name and his/her bonus:

```
scala> val empList = List(("Roy", 100), ("Sunil", 200), ("Atul", 120))
empList: List[(String, Int)] = List((Roy,100), (Sunil,200), (Atul,120))
```

Now, we need to find out the employee names whose bonus is greater than 100:

```
scala> empList filter (e => e._2 > 100) map (e => e._1)
res8: List[String] = List(Sunil, Atul)
```

All these underscores are going to make the code, well, a little unreadable. A partial function comes handy in this case:

```
scala> empList filter { case (_, bonus) => bonus > 100 } map { case(name, _) => name }
res9: List[String] = List(Sunil, Atul)
```

The preceding one-liner filters out instances that we don't care about and selects just the names for whom the bonus is greater that 100.

Here, `Filter` and `map` are passed as partial functions. However, `filter` and `map` expect a function. As `PartialFunction` is a subtype of a function, we can pass it in without any issues. Here's yet another idiom to keep in your pocket!

Visitor pattern – the Scala way

Armed with all this knowledge from the preceding sections, we can write the following sweet and succinct Scala version:

```
object FamilyAndFriends extends App {
  abstract class Friend(name: String) { // 1
    def greet(husband: Husband): Unit
    def greet(wife: Wife): Unit
  }


  case class HusbandsFriend(name: String) extends Friend(name) { // 2
    override def greet(husband: Husband): Unit = println("Hey Buddy, " +
husband.name)


    override def greet(wife: Wife): Unit = println("Hello Mrs. " + wife.
name)
  }


  abstract class FamilyMember(name: String)    // 3
  case class Husband(name: String) extends FamilyMember(name)
  case class Wife(name: String) extends FamilyMember(name)


  val husband = Husband("Ritesh")
  val wife = Wife("Nita")
  val husbandsFriend = HusbandsFriend("Prakash")


  def greetEachOther(familyMember: FamilyMember, friend: Friend) =
familyMember match { // 4
    case h: Husband => friend.greet (h) // 5
    case w: Wife => friend.greet(w)
    case _ => println("Hi")
  }


  greetEachOther(husband, husbandsFriend)
  greetEachOther(wife, husbandsFriend)
}
```

The salient points of the preceding code are as follows:

- Here, we defined the abstract `Friend` class
- We concrete instance, `HusbandsFriend`, of the `Friend` class
- Our stable hierarchy here is the `FamilyMember` abstraction, and its concrete instances, `Husband` and `Wife`, are defined just after it

The visit takes place here and greetings are exchanged. A pattern match can be matched against an object's runtime type.

We know that `FamilyMember` is `Husband`. We perform a **dynamic dispatch** to find the concrete friend. This is the same as what we have in the Java version.

The important thing is that we don't need any `accept(Friend)` call. The pattern matching allows us to do this as needed. This shows both the **Functional** and **Object-oriented** personalities of Scala to us. This dual personality is used very effectively here. This pattern will be seen again when you come to learn about the Actor paradigm.

Lifting it up

As a partial function is undefined for `some` values, how best do we deal with it? You guessed it right, we have a nice option, `Option[T]`. A `Some` value is defined, whereas a `None` is undefined. In fact, there is an `isDefined` method on `Options`. It returns `true` when invoked on `Some` and `false` on `None`.

`PartialFunction` provides the `lift` method. For a well-defined input, we get the result wrapped in `Some`. For a not so well-defined input, we get `None`. As `List[A]` is an instance of `PartialFunction`, it has a `lift()` method, as shown here:

```scala
scala> list.lift(99)
res0: Option[Int] = None
```

By lifting `PartialFunction[A, B]`, we get `Function[A, Option[B]]`.

Similarly, note the partial function syntax here:

```scala
scala> val f: PartialFunction[Int, Int] = { case i if i > 0 => i * i } //
1
f: PartialFunction[Int,Int] = <function1>
scala> f(10)
res8: Int = 100
scala> f(-1)
scala.MatchError: -1 (of class java.lang.Integer) -1
```

...

```scala
scala> f.lift(10)
res1: Option[Int] = Some(100)
res1: Option[Int] = Some(100)
scala> f.lift(-1)
res10: Option[Int] = None
```

Here is the diagrammatic representation of this example:

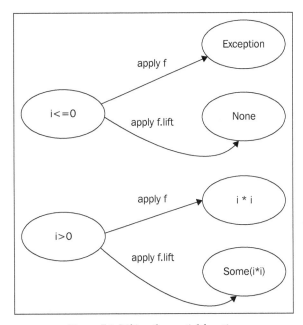

Figure 7.4 Lifting the partial function

The chain of responsibility

We looked at the command design pattern in *Chapter 1, Grokking the Functional Way*. There, the sender and executor are decoupled. Taking the idea further, we could have a pipeline of command objects that are linked together in a list. As in command, the sender submits a request. However, the request could be handled by any of the command objects in the pipeline.

We talked of moms and their kids and of kids and their mums. So the dads of the world united and started feeling left out. No worries, there is a place under the Sun for dads too! Dads have big responsibilities of dealing with stuff, in a world-wise fashion. In a family, thus, we have roles and responsibilities. Dads are used to fix broken things around the house, cut firewood, hunt, fish, and sow the land. Moms cook, sew, and keep the house clean. Kids have a big business of growing up, and when they get some time away from their never-ending pranks, they study and play. And in an effort to make themselves useful, they mess things up, which again will have to be fixed by the moms and dads. Every mom knows she would rather cook food instead of cutting wood. On the other hand, a dad knows that it is tough to sew up a torn button. Kids can lend a hand and help with walking the dogs. So everyone in the family knows what each family member can do—or rather not do. Tasks line up every day and the family as a whole intuitively handles or passes on these as appropriate.

The family members could be thought of as forming a chain of tasks that each one is responsible for. The chain, as a whole, is responsible for handling those myriad tasks. The beauty of this arrangement is that if a grand mom comes to stay for a while and loves to water plants, she can pick up some gardening tasks! So now we have a chain wherein multiple responsibilities are handled. This chain of responsibilities pattern decouples the handler from a task pretty nicely, as shown in the following code:

```
public abstract class FamilyMember {
  protected final FamilyMember next; // 1

  public FamilyMember(final FamilyMember next) {
    super();
    this.next = next;
  }

  public abstract boolean canHandle(Task task);
  public abstract void handleIt(Task task);

  public void doSomeWork(Task task) {
    if (canHandle(task)) { // 2
      handleIt(task);
    } else if (next != null) {
      next.doSomeWork(task);
    }
```

```
    }

}

public class Task {
  private final String name;

  public String getName() {
    return name;
  }

  public Task(String name) {
  this.name = name;
  }

  private boolean containsOneOf(String... phraseList) {
    for (String phrase : phraseList) {
    if (contains(phrase)) {
      return true;
      }
    }
    return false;
  }

  private boolean contains(String phrase) {
  return name.toLowerCase().contains(phrase);
  }

  public boolean needsHardLabor() {
  return containsOneOf("wood", "Fell", "hunt");
  }

  public boolean needsHouseHoldSkills() {
    return containsOneOf("sew", "cook");
```

```
    }

  public boolean isLightWeight() {
    return containsOneOf("dog", "cat", "playground");
  }
}


public class Dad extends FamilyMember {

  public Dad(FamilyMember next) {
    super(next);
  }

  @Override
  public boolean canHandle(Task task) {
    return task.needsHardLabor(); // 3
  }

  @Override
  public void handleIt(Task task) { // 4
    System.out.println("Dad Handling: " + task.getName());
  }

}


public class Mom extends FamilyMember {

  public Mom(FamilyMember next) {
    super(next);
  }

  @Override
  public boolean canHandle(Task task) {
    return task.needsHouseHoldSkills();
```

```
}

@Override
public void handleIt(Task task) {
  System.out.println("Mom Handling: " + task.getName());
}

}
```

The code for the Kid class is not shown here, as it is on the similar lines. Refer to the book's source code for more details.

The salient points of the preceding code are as follows:

- The FamilyMember class holds the next member in a chain.
- If the current member can handle the task, it does so. Otherwise, it hands over the task to the next member in the chain.
- In the chain, a dad (Dad) knows what he can handle and handles the task.
- A mom (Mom) knows what she can handle and handles the task.

Here is the UML diagram showing how the pieces fit together:

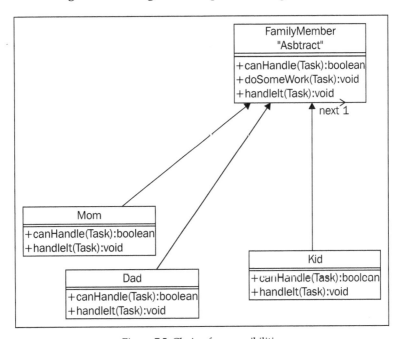

Figure 7.5: Chain of responsibilities

Scalaish Chain Of Responsibilities

Here is how we would express this chain in Scala. The chain will be formed by partial functions that are chained together with the `orElse` method:

```scala
object ChainOfResponsibility extends App {
  case class Task(description: String) // 1

  type TaskHandler = PartialFunction[Task, Unit] // 2

  def canHandle(phrases: List[String], task: Task) = // 3
    phrases exists (task.description.toLowerCase.contains(_))

  def handleIt(name: String, task: Task) = println(s"${name} Handling: "
+ task.description)

  val dad: TaskHandler = { // 4
    case task: Task if canHandle(List("wood", "hunt"), task) =>
handleIt("Dad", task)
  }

  val mom: TaskHandler = { // 5
    case task: Task if canHandle(List("sew", "cook"), task) =>
handleIt("Mom", task)
  }

  val kid: TaskHandler = {
    case task: Task if canHandle(List("dog", "cat"), task) =>
handleIt("Kid", task)
  }

  val f = dad orElse mom orElse kid // 6

  f(Task("feed the cat")) // 7

  val taskList = List("sew up a shirt button",
```

```
    "Walk the Dog", "cut some firewood", "feed the cat")


  taskList map (Task(_)) map f // 8
}
```

The code is expressive, to the point, and pretty succinct when compared to the equivalent Java version.

The salient features of the preceding code are as follows:

- Our task is expressed as a `case class`.
- We can use the type alias instead of the verbose `PartialFunction` type.
- The `canHandle()` method for every member knows about, defining tasks the member can handle.
- Our dad with his responsibilities is expressed as a partial function.
- Our mom with her responsibilities is expressed as a partial function. The kid follows on the next line.
- Our chain of responsibilities is joined with the `orElse` statement. So if dad cannot do some task, it is given to the mom. If mom can't handle it, it goes to the kid.
- An example invocation, the task is to feed the cat, and only the kid handles it.
- Then, we go over a list of phrases that are expressed as `List[String]`. Each list element is converted to a task, and then, f is invoked on each of these tasks.

Here is how this example looks pictorially:

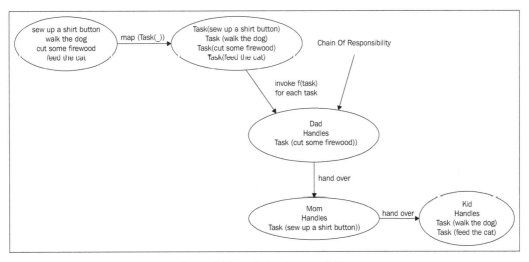

Figure 7.6: The chain of responsibility

Chains are everywhere

The underlying theme behind this design is object composition. We are essentially composing a pipeline of handlers. The objects (dad, mom, and kid) are chained together. We can also add more objects, such as grandmother, grandfather, uncles, and aunts to the mix. This is similar to the Unix way of chaining small utilities together to form a pipeline. In functional programming, you have a lot of small functions that all do one specific thing, and they do it well. Unix pipelines really are a filtering mechanism where we chain filters together. Filters are blissfully unaware of the pipeline. Each filter simply reads a text stream from an input, works on it, and outputs some text. The shell connects the filters together. This allows us to connect filters in any way of our choosing. Note the similarity in the following Scala and Shell snippets:

```
scala> List("filtering", "is", "great", "fun") filter(
  _.length >= 3 )
```

versus

```
~> echo "filtering

is

great

fun" | awk 'length >= 3'
```

We will be seeing many examples of compositions as the book progresses further.

In the chain of responsibility pattern, one of the object handles the request. On the other hand, in pipes and filters, every command in the pipeline participates in the overall processing. For more information, refer to http://stackoverflow.com/questions/27174703/difference-between-pipe-filter-and-chain-of-responsibility for more on the differences.

Match and mismatch – the collect idiom

There is one catch with our chain implementation, though. If the chain cannot handle the task, it throws throws an exception. For example, let's create a task to try feeding the parrot:

```
scala> f(Task("feed the parrot"))
scala.MatchError: Task(feed the parrot) (of class Task)
  at scala.PartialFunction$$anon$1.apply(PartialFunction.scala:253)
... etc... etc...
```

The chain could not handle this. The task traveled down the chain and reached the kid. As the kid is also not programmed to handle it, we get an error. `PartialFunction` provides a convenience method, `isDefined()`, for such cases:

```scala
scala>   if (f.isDefinedAt(Task("feed the parrot"))) {
     |       f(Task("feed the parrot"))
     |   }

scala>   if (f.isDefinedAt(Task("feed the dog"))) {
     |       f(Task("feed the dog"))
     |   }
Kid Handling: feed the dog
```

Now, when the combinators are chained, it would be cool if the isDefinedAt is used behind the scenes. So in case a partial function is not defined for the input, we should skip it and try the next function (if any).

```scala
scala> val list = List("Feed the parrot", "feed the cat", "sew the button")
list: List[String] = List(Feed the parrot, feed the cat, sew the button)

scala> list map (Task(_))
res7: List[Task] = List(Task(Feed the parrot), Task(feed the cat), Task(sew the button))

scala> list map (Task(_)) map f
scala.MatchError: Task(Feed the parrot) (of class Task)
… etc... etc...
```

We need to just use `collect` instead of `map` and it works. A `collect` first checks whether the function is defined for the input:

```scala
scala> list map (Task(_)) collect f
Kid Handling: feed the cat
Mom Handling: sew the button
```

So now we know the difference between `map` and `collect`. By the way, there is one more way to weed out the unsupported tasks:

```scala
scala> list map (Task(_)) flatMap { x => f.lift(x) }
Kid Handling: feed the cat
Mom Handling: sew the button
res13: Lisnit] = List((), ())
```

As we know, lifting the partial function gives us either Some(String) or None. The flatMap filters our the None elements and flattens the **Some** elements.

Here is another example in a similar vein:

```scala
scala> val listOfAnys = List("x", 33, 21, "y", 55, 2.0, "z")
listOfAnys: List[Any] = List(x, 33, 21, y, 55, 2.0, z)

scala> listOfAnys collect { case s: String => s }
res12: List[String] = List(x, y, z)
```

This is a **typed pattern** match, as shown in the preceding example. The pattern matches only for string elements so that they are collected and returned.

Summary

In this chapter, we looked at two very important concepts in Scala, namely pattern matching and partial functions. We saw many examples where pattern matching comes handy, and its application to get the double dispatch works for us. We implemented the chain of responsibilities design pattern in Java. Partial functions are a very useful concept in their own right, and we saw how to implement the chain of responsibilities using partial functions in Scala. Along the way, we looked at the collect functions. The stage is set now for you to get into the thick of functional programming. We have already briefly touched upon the theme of composition and how to create a pipeline. In the upcoming chapter, we will see various functional combinators and put them to use in order to compose large behavior from smaller parts. So, tighten your seat belts, and let's fly into the functional wonderland!

8
Traversals – Mapping/ Filtering/Folding/Reducing

We, software developers, love creating data structures and traversing them. We traverse structures so as to visit elements therein. A traversal typically uses a loop.

However, doesn't writing a `for` loop (or a `foreach` loop) seem like a routine job, also known as a boilerplate? I would rather concentrate on the element and let the language figure out and write the looping for me. Again, what I wish to do with each element depends on the context (that is, it varies). On the other hand, writing a `for` loop seems like typing the same chars again and again.

IDEs like Eclipse provide helpful completions for such routine and boring stuff. However, could we have the loop abstracted away, and instead let it happen behind the scenes? Answer: yes, use the combinators. In fact, we have already used some in earlier chapters, `foreach` and `map`.

Combinators and functions come together and make the magic happen. Using combinators helps cut down on repetitive looping code. The code becomes small, succinct, and more readable.

We will be looking at multiple flavors of combinators. Walking through a simple example, we will see how powerful combinators are. We will look at each combinator in detail and understand where those apply. We will look at the flatMap in greater detail and see how this combinator helps realize the monad pattern in Scala.

Iterating the Scala way

In the imperative Java world, we are used to writing loops. For example:

```java
int[] arr = new int[10];
for (int i = 0; i < 10; ++i) {
    arr[i] = arr[i] + 1;
}
System.out.println(Arrays.toString(arr));
```

This changes the array *in place* (that is, the original data structure is being mutated). The Scala way is:

```scala
scala> val list = List.fill(10)(0)
list: List[Int] = List(0, 0, 0, 0, 0, 0, 0, 0, 0, 0)
scala> list map (a => a + 1) foreach { a => print(" " + a) }
 1 1 1 1 1 1 1 1 1 1
scala> list
res3: List[Int] = List(0, 0, 0, 0, 0, 0, 0, 0, 0, 0)
```

Instead of coding the loop, we *pass in* a function to a construct, to building blocks called combinators. These building blocks aka combinators allow themselves to be composed into a higher-level combinator. These combinators allow you to think in terms of higher-level operations and their interactions, instead of low-level details. This is an example of the power of higher order functions.

Also note that the original list remains *unchanged!* The output of a combinator is a brand new list. We have already touched on this immutable way of things, as well as structural sharing. Being immutable, we have less moving parts to worry about.

For example, consider the following UNIX command line:

```
/home/atul> sed -ne '/\(.\)\1/p' bigfile.txt | wc -l
   14343
```

This pipeline does quite a lot–sed opens up a text file, reads the lines one by one, and outputs lines in which there are two (or more) of the same characters side by side. These lines are counted by the word counter program wc. If you put this pipeline in a shell script, or a shell function, you have just created a new building block!

The Scala way is functional. We make each element of the list go through a function, a => a+1, via the map invocation, creating a **new list**. Each element of this new list is printed by another function, a => print(" " + a). We make this pipe lining happen with the help of combinators, like map and foreach. This is a very different (and succinct) way of looping.

Note the Java version. We are really interested in incrementing each element, and then printing all of the array. At the same time, we need to code the loop and make sure the loop does not overshoot the array. This is the boilerplate that Scala helps eliminate. Just concentrate on what you wish to do (that is. functions) and a side-effect free way (functions again). (Note: The function given to the `foreach` combinator is not side-effect free).

Another important theme is the **pipelining**. We take the result of the map combinator and pass it on to the `foreach`.

We will run through an example, comparing and contrasting the various ways to iterate and combine expressions.

A validation problem

We need to validate incoming data. Consider an online banking application. Users have already registered and their passwords are with the bank.

The bank security team changed their requirements, so each password must now have at least six characters and a mix of upper and lowercase letters. We need to pull out the already existing passwords and see if these qualify with the new rules.

So, given a list of password strings, we need to compute a corresponding list of Booleans that will return true if the password qualifies, and otherwise false. In other words, given this list of password strings, we need a `Tuple2(List[String],` `List[Boolean])`.

Setting the stage

The following is the example list of passwords:

```scala
scala> val passwords = List("oddoddboy@thedoor", "likelynew",
"alwaysThinkOfMyself", "naughty")
passwords: List[String] = List(oddoddboy@thedoor, likelynew,
alwaysThinkOfMyself, naughty)
```

Let's define our length-checking function as shown:

```scala
scala> def lengthGreaterThan(minLen: Int)(s: String) = s.length >= minLen
lengthGreaterThan: (minLen: Int)(s: String)Boolean


scala> val validatePasswdLen = lengthGreaterThan(6) _
validatePasswdLen: String => Boolean = <function1>
```

We are on known grounds. This is currying at work:

```
scala> validatePasswdLen("hi")
res0: Boolean = false


scala> validatePasswdLen("hithere")
res1: Boolean = true
```

Next, let's write the functions for character validation:

```
scala> def containsChar(c: Char, s: String) = s.contains(c)
containsChar: (c: Char, s: String)Boolean


scala> def containsOneOf(set: Seq[Char])(s: String) = set exists( c =>
containsChar(c, s))
containsOneOf: (set: String)(s: String)Boolean
scala> val containsUpperCaseChar = containsOneOf('A' to 'Z') _
containsUpperCaseChar: String => Boolean = <function1>


scala> val containsLowerCaseChar = containsOneOf('a' to 'z') _
containsLowerCaseChar: String => Boolean = <function1>
```

The expression `('a' to 'z').toList.mkString` results in the string `abcdefghijklmnopqrstuvwxyz`. The a to z is a character range. We will deal with ranges when we come to the `for` comprehension. The range object is converted to a list and then a string is made out of it:

```
scala> containsLowerCaseChar("Hi")
res0: Boolean = true


scala> containsLowerCaseChar("HEY")
res1: Boolean = false
```

Now, we need to combine these three functions, namely, `validatePasswdLen`, `containsLowerChar`, and `containsUpperChar`, and apply them to **each** element of the input word list. The expected output for our passwords list is:

```
List((oddoddboy@thedoor,false), (likelynew,false),
(alwaysThinkOfMyself,true), (naughty,false))
```

First cut–using arrays

Let's try solving this using arrays:

```scala
scala> val arr = Array.fill(passwords.length)(false)
```

```scala
scala> passwords.indices.foreach { i =>
     |     arr(i) = validatePasswdLen(passwords(i)) && containsLowerCaseChar(passwords(i)) && containsUpperCaseChar(passwords(i))
     | }
```

We iterate over the list, using `foreach`. The `foreach` combinator takes a function, passing in every element as an argument to the function. `Foreach` returns nothing. Even if you try returning a value, you get back a unit:

```scala
scala> val p = passwords.indices.foreach { i => i + 1 }
p: Unit = ()
```

We are using `foreach` for its side effects. We take each element in the list, invoke each function on it, and store the result in the array `arr`:

```scala
scala> (passwords zip arr)
res2: List[(String, Boolean)] = List((oddoddboy@thedoor,false),
(likelynew,false), (alwaysThinkOfMyself,true), (naughty,false))
```

The **Zip** creates a list of tuples. It creates the tuple elements by combining elements from each list as shown in the following figure:

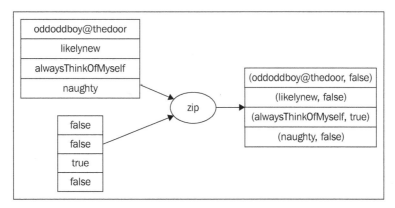

Figure 8.1: Zipping up two collections

This code works; however, it has a problem. Accessing random elements of a list is not efficient. To reach the 99th element of a list, the code can't jump to it directly. It first hops to the 0th element, then to the 1st element, then to the 2nd, until it reaches the 99th node.

We could have applied `http://refactoring.com/catalog/extractVariable. html` to extract the `passwords(i)` expression into a temporary variable. This would cache the list value. Instead of traversing the list again and again, we traverse only once and save the value for subsequent use. It is better but still suboptimal.

Indexing into an array is alright, though, so the `arr(i)` expression on the left-hand side is fine.

We can eliminate indexing into the list, however. Here is an improved version:

```scala
scala> var i = 0
i: Int = 0

scala> passwords.foreach { w =>
     |    array(i) = validatePasswdLen(w) && containsLowerCaseChar(w) &&
containsUpperCaseChar(w)
     |    i += 1
     | }
```

Voilà! We have eliminated list indexing! This is a much better version. Sporting an index with list elements is commonly needed, so Scala provides `zipWithIndex`.

Now, we can rewrite it as shown here:

```scala
scala> passwords.zipWithIndex foreach  { case (w, i) =>
     |    array(i) = validatePasswdLen(w) && containsLowerCaseChar(w) &&
containsUpperCaseChar(w)
     | }
```

We have eliminated the `var`! We now have the index and use it for the array access.

Second cut–using a map

It seems there is a more functional way to solve the above. We can use a map instead of coding an explicit `foreach` loop.

A map works with both a collection and function. It invokes the given function on each element of the collection and returns a new collection with the mapped elements as a result.

For example, we can make a list of string greetings uppercase, as shown:

```
scala> val greetings = List("hello", "salaam", "namaste", "salud",
"bonjour")
greetings: List[String] = List(hello, salaam, namaste, salud, bonjour)
```

```
scala> greetings map (x => x.toUpperCase)
res9: List[String] = List(HELLO, SALAAM, NAMASTE, SALUD, BONJOUR)
```

The original list is left untouched.

Let's compose our functions together so we can use them easily:

```
scala> val checker = (w: String) => (w, validatePasswdLen(w) &&
containsLowerCaseChar(w) && containsUpperCaseChar(w))
checker: String => (String, Boolean)
```

```
scala> passwords.map (x => checker(x))
res7: List[(String, Boolean)] = List((oddoddboy@thedoor,false),
(likelynew,false), (alwaysThinkOfMyself,true), (naughty,false))
```

This is really a nice version. The `map` combinator invokes the anonymous function, x => `checker(x)` on each element of the `passwords` list, resulting in a new list:

```
scala> passwords.map (x => checker(x)).unzip
res6: (List[String], List[Boolean]) = (List(oddoddboy@thedoor, likelynew,
alwaysThinkOfMyself, naughty),List(false, false, true, false))
```

The `unzip` takes the list of tuples and creates two separate lists.

Pictorially, it looks exactly opposite to the preceding zipping process:

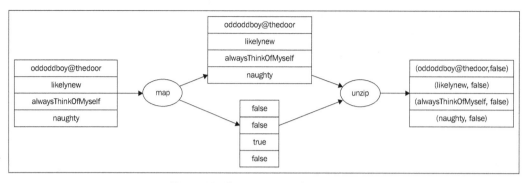

Figure 8.2: The mapping and unzipping

Third cut–using a for expression

Scala has `for` expressions, and they return values. For example:

```
scala> for (p <- List(1,2,3)) yield(p+1)
res8: List[Int] = List(2, 3, 4)
```

The clause p ← List(1,2,3) is a generator. The variable p is set to each element of the list, yielded by the expression. Using a `for` expression, our version looks like:

```
scala> val result = for (w <- passwords) yield checker(w)
scala> result.unzip
```

Shortening it, we get the following smaller version:

```
scala> (for (w <- passwords) yield checker(w)).unzip
```

This is very similar to the preceding map version. We will soon see how similar they are.

Fourth cut–using foldLeft

We could use `foldLeft` instead. Here is how `foldLeft` works:

```
scala> val l = List(7,8,9)
l: List[Int] = List(7, 8, 9)
scala> l.foldLeft(0)(_+_)
res1: Int = 24
```

The `foldLeft` method starts with an accumulator, which is initialized to `0` in this case, and a collection. It adds the first value of the collection to the accumulator, and that becomes the next accumulator. The process is repeated for all remaining elements of the collection. The preceding `foldLeft` does the summation `0+7+8+9` and gives back `24`.

To press `foldLeft` in service, we need to tweak the definition of the `checker` function a bit:

```scala
scala> def checker = (w: String) => (validatePasswdLen(w) &&
containsLowerCaseChar(w) && containsUpperCaseChar(w))

checker: String => Boolean

scala> passwords.foldLeft(List.empty[String], List.empty[Boolean])((b, a)
=> (a :: b._1, checker(a) :: b._2))
```

This, too, is a very succinct version, using just one combinator, `foldLeft`.

Fifth cut–using andThen

Scala gives us `andThen`. This combinator combines functions by taking one parameter–that is a `Functional`.

Please visit the following link for more information:
`http://www.scala-lang.org/api/current/index.html#scala.Function1`

Here is an illustrative example:

```scala
scala> val p1 = (x: Int) => x * 2
p: Int => Int = <function1>


scala> val p2 = (x: Int) => x + 1
p2: Int => Int = <function1>


scala> val p3 = (x: Int) => x + 2
p3: Int => Int = <function1>


scala> val p = p1 andThen p2 andThen p3
```

```
p: Int => Int = <function1>
```

```
scala> p(10)
res1: Int = 23
```

The example is explained with the help of following figure:

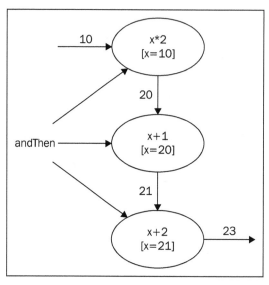

Figure 8.3: chaining function with andThen

So, `f` is realized by **composing** `f1`, `f2`, and `f3` together. To solve our problem, we can press `andThen` into service as shown here:

```
scala> type PassWdChecker = (String, Boolean) => (String, Boolean)
defined type alias PassWdChecker
```

We then define a type alias. This helps with readability:

```
scala> val f1: PassWdChecker = (x: String, b: Boolean) => (x,
containsLowerCaseChar(x))
f1: PassWdChecker = <function2>
```

```
scala> val f2: PassWdChecker = (x: String, b: Boolean) => (x,
containsUpperCaseChar(x))
f2: PassWdChecker = <function2>
```

```
scala> val f3: PassWdChecker = (x: String, b: Boolean) => (x,
validatePasswdLen(x))
```

```
f3: PassWdChecker = <function2>
```

```
scala> val f = f1.tupled andThen f2.tupled andThen f3.tupled
f: ((String, Boolean)) => (String, Boolean) = <function1>
```

We have functions f1, f2, and f3 each taking and returning a PassWdChecker. As all three are of the type Function2 (they take two parameters), the andThen method is not available. So, we convert each to a Function1 form by calling the tupled method.

The tupled method converts the two-parameter version into a one-parameter version by stashing the parameters into a tuple and accepting that instead.

This conversion enables us to use the andThen method. take a look at the following figure as an example:

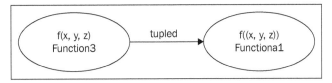

Figure 8.4: Tupling a multi-parameter function

A nice Scala convenience is at work, making it easier to call this tupled version:

```
scala> def m(x: (Int, Int)) = x._1 * x._2
m: (x: (Int, Int))Int
```

```
scala> m(2, 3)
res1: Int = 6
```

Scala coalesces multiple function call parameters into a tuple.

Sixth cut–using compose

This is similar to the andThen version. The difference is the order in which the composed functions get called.

Applying compose to functions p1, p2, and p3 above, the composition looks like the following:

```
scala> val p1 = (x: Int) => x * 2
p1: Int => Int = <function1>
```

```
scala> val p2 = (x: Int) => x + 1
```

```
p2: Int => Int = <function1>

scala> val p3 = (x: Int) => x + 2
p3: Int => Int = <function1>

scala> val p = p1 compose p2 compose p3
p: Int => Int = <function1>

scala> p(10)
res0: Int = 26
```

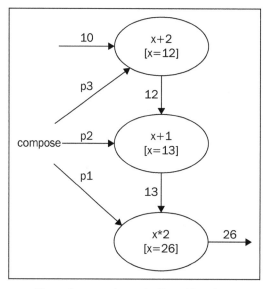

Figure 5–composing a pipeline of functions

So, in composing functions `f1`, `f2`, and `f3`, the checking is done in reverse order compared to the `andThen` version:

```
scala> val f = f1.tupled compose f2.tupled compose f3.tupled
f: ((String, Boolean)) => (String, Boolean) = <function1>

scala> f("HTHERe", false)
res1: (String, Boolean) = (HTHERe,true)
```

In this particular case, the calling order of functions does not matter, because if any one function fails, the entire validation will also fail. So, either `andThen` or `compose` would work well for us.

Foreach–sugary sweetener

We briefly touched on the `for` expression. We also noted how the `for` expressions are similar to the map version. In fact, the Scala compiler translates the `for` expression into a form using map, flatMap, and filter. The following are how the forms of the expression are translated.

One generator

This is a simple case that can be readily translated into a form that uses a map:

```
scala> for (p <- List(1,2,3)) yield(p+1)
res10: List[Int] = List(2, 3, 4)
```

Gets translated into the following:

```
scala> List(1,2,3) map (p => p + 1)
res11: List[Int] = List(2, 3, 4)
```

A generator and a filter

Let's try printing pretty numbers from a list, such that each number is divisible by 3:

```
scala> val p = (1 to 20).toList
p: List[Int] = List(1, 2, 3, 4, 5, 6, 7, 8, 9, 10, 11, 12, 13, 14, 15,
16, 17, 18, 19, 20)
scala> for (k <- p if k % 3 == 0) yield("<" + k + ">")
res12: List[String] = List(<3>, <6>, <9>, <12>, <15>, <18>)
```

This expression gets translated as below. Note that I can always rewrite the `for` expression by replacing the `if` element with a call to a filter:

```
scala> for (k <- p filter(x => x % 3 == 0)) yield("<" + k + ">")
```

As the `filter` expression will result in a collection, we can use the map to work on the **filtered collection**:

```
scala> p filter (_ % 3 == 0) map (x => "<" + x + ">")
res14: List[String] = List(<3>, <6>, <9>, <12>, <15>, <18>)
```

If there are two filters, the same translation is done one after another. For example:

```
scala> for (k <- p if k % 3 == 0; if k % 2 == 0) yield("<" + k + ">")
res15: List[String] = List(<6>, <12>, <18>)
```

Is translated into the following:

```
scala> p filter (_ % 3 == 0) filter (_ % 2 == 0) map (x => "<" + x + ">")
res16: List[String] = List(<6>, <12>, <18>)
```

The conditions in `for` comprehension are converted into a call to `withFilter` instead of `filter`. If `filter` were used, it would create an intermediate collection for each condition applied. `withFilter` is a lazy combinator. The above discussion mentions `filter` for an ease of understanding.

The `withFilter` combinator delays evaluation until absolutely necessary. We learned about lazy evaluation and views in *Chapter 4, Lazy Sequences - Being Lazy, Being Good.* For a chain of `withFilter` calls, each `withFilter` invocation passes down a view to the next `withFilter` in line.

Only when the element is necessary are all the filters invoked.

Please see the following websites for more information:

`http://tataryn.net/whats-in-a-scala-for-comprehension/`

`https://gist.github.com/ruippeixotog/25110822eba d1217adc8)`

Two generators

Generating a cartesian product of two (or more) vectors is pretty easy:

```
scala> val m = (1 to 3).toList
m: List[Int] = List(1, 2, 3)
scala> val n = (1 to 3).toList
n: List[Int] = List(1, 2, 3)

scala> for (i <- m; j <- n) yield (i + "" + j)
res17: List[String] = List(11, 12, 13, 21, 22, 23, 31, 32, 33)
```

Could we translate it with two maps? Let's try the following command:

```
scala> m map (i =>
     |   n map (j =>
     |     i + "" + j))
res18: List[List[String]] = List(List(11, 12, 13), List(21, 22, 23),
List(31, 32, 33))
```

We are pretty close, but not quite there. We need to flatten out the list of lists. There is already a combinator, flatMap, we can use instead of the first map:

```scala
scala> m flatMap (i =>
     |    n map (j =>
     |    i + "" + j))
res19: List[String] = List(11, 12, 13, 21, 22, 23, 31, 32, 33)
```

This is the translation done by the Scala compiler for more than one generators in the for expression.

What happens when we have more than two generator expressions? Let's check with the following commands:

```scala
scala> val o = List(1,2)
o: List[Int] = List(1, 2)
scala> for (i <- m; j <- n; k <- o) yield (i + "" + j + "" + k)
res21: List[String] = List(111, 112, 121, 122, 131, 132, 211, 212, 221,
222, 231, 232, 311, 312, 321, 322, 331, 332)
```

This for expression is translated into the following:

```scala
scala> m flatMap (i =>
     |    n flatMap (j =>
     |       o map (k =>
     |       i + "" + j + "" + k)))
res23: List[String] = List(111, 112, 121, 122, 131, 132, 211, 212, 221,
222, 231, 232, 311, 312, 321, 322, 331, 332)
```

It is easier to see why we need a series of flatMaps. Each internal combinator results in a list, and the result needs to be flattened out. Try replacing the flatMap calls to a map, and the understanding will click in. Refer to he the following figure as an example:

Figure 8.6: chaining flatMaps and a map

There is a chaining of computations at work here. You are looking at a list monad.

Monads

In the above, `flatMap` binds stuff together. All the combinator blocks are closure blocks. The `map` block, for example, is accessing variables from its enclosing scopes. And all blocks are returning back a list of strings.

What does a `flatMap` do? It maps and then flattens the result. For example, the following is a way to pick up numbers from `List[Any]`. Using a map does not fully cut it:

```scala
scala> val l = List(1, "this", 2, 4.4, 'c')
l: List[Any] = List(1, this, 2, 4.4, c)


scala> l map {
     |     case i: Int => Some(i)
     |     case _ => None
     | }
res0: List[Option[Int]] = List(Some(1), None, Some(2), None, None)
```

We just need the numbers; however, we get them wrapped up in `Some` or we get them wrapped up in `None`. We have already seen both how we could collect and a partial function for picking up numbers:

```scala
scala> l flatMap {
     |     case i: Int => Some(i)
     |     case _ => None
     | }
res1: List[Int] = List(1, 2)
```

So, `flatMap` does both the **mapping** (invoking the provided function, passing in each element) and the **flattening** of the result (extracting out the values from `Some` and throwing out the `None`).

Lists are monads and so are options. Can we mix two monadic types? Let's try the following:

```scala
scala> val m = (1 to 9).toList
m: List[Int] = List(1, 2, 3, 4, 5, 6, 7, 8, 9)


scala> val n = Map(1 -> 7, 15 -> 11, 9 -> 22)
```

```
n: scala.collection.immutable.Map[Int,Int] = Map(1 -> 7, 15 -> 11, 9 ->
22)
```

```
scala> for {
     |    i <- m
     |    k <- n.get(i)
     | } yield k
res0: List[Int] = List(7, 22)
```

We know by now that we can rewrite the de-sugared version as follows:

```
scala> m flatMap { i =>
     |    n.get(i) map { k =>
     |      k
     |    }
     | }
res1: List[Int] = List(7, 22)
```

So, what makes a list or an option a monad?

Monads are containers. They support higher order functions and can be combined together. We can provide these operations on our types and use the `for` comprehension to manipulate them.

Reduce

Just like `fold`, there is a `reduce` combinator. And there are two versions: `reduceLeft` and `reduceRight`. Here is an example:

```
scala> val l = List(1,2,3)
l: List[Int] = List(1, 2, 3)
```

```
scala> l reduceLeft { (acc, n) => acc + n }
res4: Int = 6
```

In `fold`, we provide the initial value for the accumulator. However, here the accumulator is set to the first value of the collection.

If there is no first value, the reduce will fail as shown here:

```
scala> List[Int]() reduceLeft { (acc, n) => acc + n }
java.lang.UnsupportedOperationException: empty.reduceLeft
```

On the other hand, if invoked on an empty collection, `fold` returns the initial value itself:

```scala
scala> val l = List[Int]()
l: List[Int] = List()
scala> l.fold(0) { (acc, n) => acc + n }
res17: Int = 0
```

Having got our feet wet, here is an interesting example that tells us some more about `reduce`. We will also see what the differences are between the left and right versions of `reduce`. Let's say we need to print a list of numbers, separated with a $-$ sign:

```scala
scala> val nums = (1 to 10).toList map { _.toString }
nums: List[String] = List(1, 2, 3, 4, 5, 6, 7, 8, 9, 10)

scala> val s = nums.reduceLeft { (acc, n) =>
     |    acc + " - " + n
     | }
s: String = 1 - 2 - 3 - 4 - 5 - 6 - 7 - 8 - 9 - 10
```

Let's try it on a huge list of 20,000 elements:

```scala
scala> val nums = (1 to 20000).toList map { _.toString }
nums: List[String] = List(1, 2, 3, 4,…)
scala> val s = nums.reduceLeft { (acc, n) =>
     |    acc + " - " + n
     | }
s: String = 1 - 2 - 3 - 4 - 5 - 6 - 7 - 8 - 9 - 10 - 11 - 12 - 13 - 14 -
15 - 16 - 17 - 18 - 19 - 20 - 21 - 22…
```

As a bonus, this works pretty nicely as for a single value; no separator is printed. Try it out!

Now, replace the `reduceLeft` call with `reduceRight`. For the list with 20 elements, it works fine. But for the big list of 20,000 elements, we get a `StackOverflowError`:

```scala
scala> val s = nums.reduceRight { (acc, n) =>
     |    acc + ", " + n
     | }
java.lang.StackOverflowError
   at scala.collection.LinearSeqOptimized$class.
reduceRight(LinearSeqOptimized.scala:142)
   at scala.collection.immutable.List.reduceRight(List.scala:84)
```

Hark back, dear reader, to our discussion on the accumulator idiom, tail recursion, and **tail call optimization (TCO)**. The left version can use TCO and hence gets rewritten to use loops. On the other hand, the right version cannot use TCO.

The left version goes from the first element to the last. The right version goes the other way, from the last element to the first (remember, it is reduceRight).

Here is what reduceLeft would look like:

```scala
import scala.annotation.tailrec

object ReduceLeft extends App {

  def reduceLeft(1: List[String], f: (String, String) => String) = {
    @tailrec
    def reduceIt(acc: String, list: List[String]) : String = list match
{
      case Nil => acc
      case x :: xs => reduceIt(f(acc, x), xs)
    }
    reduceIt(1(0), 1.drop(1)) // 1
  }

  val nums = (1 to 20).toList map { _.toString }

  def f(acc: String, s: String) = s"(${acc} - ${s})"

  val result = reduceLeft(nums, f) // 2

  println(result)
}
```

We have seen most of these concepts before—please refer back to *Chapter 3, Recursion and Chasing Your Own Tail.* in case you need to jog your memory.

The standard library's reduceLeft looks different. Please see the following documentation:

https://github.com/scala/scala/blob/v2.11.7/src/library/scala/collection/TraversableOnce.scala#L1

The salient points for the preceding code are as follows:

- We call the internal workhorse function, which employs the accumulator idiom. The accumulator is initialized to the first element of the list. It is clear now why `reduce` cannot work with empty collections. The `l(0)` call will fail with an empty list.

- We call `reduceLeft` and pass in `f`. The compiler converts the `f` method into a function for us, the so-called eta expansion.

Pictorially, here is the processing order. Note the left-to-right accumulation:

$$(((1+"-"+2)+"-"+3)+"-"+4)$$

Figure 8.7: reduceLeft processing order

Our `reduceRight` would look like:

```
object ReduceRight extends App {
  def reduceRight(l: List[String], f: (String, String) => String): String
= l match {
    case Nil => throw new IllegalArgumentException("Bad List") // 1
    case y :: Nil => y // 2
    case x :: xs => f(x, reduceRight(xs, f)) // 3
  }

  val nums = (1 to 3).toList map { _.toString }

  def f(s: String, acc: String) = s"(${s} - ${acc})"

  val result = reduceRight(nums, f)

  println(result)
}
```

The salient points for the preceding code are as follows:

- We cannot work on empty lists.
- If the list has a single element, then `reduceRight` returns that element.
- The `f` is always evaluated on the right elements first. We need to hold on to all the left elements in the meantime. This costs us an expensive stack frames and hence, we get the stack overflow error for large lists. Note also the ordering of the evaluation is right first.

Note that we could simply have reversed the list and called `reduceLeft` on it! This is what the Scala library's `reduceRight` does. Please see the following documentation for more information:

```
https://github.com/scala/scala/blob/v2.11.7/src/library/scala/
collection/TraversableOnce.scala#L193
```

Our version could do with a bit of refactoring. We are repeatedly passing in the same `f` in the recursive call. This refactoring is left as an exercise.

Pictorially, here is the processing order. Note the right-to-left accumulation:

$$(1+"-"+(2+"-"+(3+"-"+4)))$$

Figure 7.8: `reduceRight` processing order

Summary

We had a whirlwind tour of traversals in this chapter. We looked at functional combinators and how looping is way different from the traditional Java `for` loop. We also played with many examples of `map`, `flatMap`, `filter`, `reduce`, `zip`, and `fold`.

Scala `for` comprehension is a syntactic sugar that hides the complexity arising out of combining combinators. A running validation example delved into the nitty-gritty of the de-sugaring of the `for` comprehension.

This know-how prepared us to better appreciate `flatMap`, the glue that binds a pipeline of computations, aka the monad pattern. We saw how the `for` comprehension realizes monad and what happens behind the scenes. In addition, we had a detailed look at the `reduce` combinator and its left and right variants. A peek behind the curtain showed us the differences between `reduceLeft` and `reduceRight`.

This is the functional style where we could compose pure functions and reason better and at a higher level of abstraction. Pure functions and combinators vastly reduce the boilerplate and promote immutability.

All this information prepares us, my dear reader, to take the next ambitious steps in looking at higher order functions. We have already had a taste of this in this chapter however, the next chapter will help you appreciate the power higher order functions give us. On to it!

9
Higher Order Functions

In the last chapter, we saw how the use of combinators simplifies code. We just have to pass in functions and not worry about the boilerplate of writing loops or creating pipelines.

The idea behind all this is that **higher order** functions can take other functions as parameters, return a function as a result, or do both. In Scala, as we already know, functions are first-class citizens. This is a rather neat idea, as we will soon see.

In this chapter, we will start with the strategy pattern and see the Java implementation. Then, we will change gears and see how this pattern is really not needed when you talk about Scala. This is largely the effect of being able to send across functions and function literals. Once we get used to passing around functions, we will look at three patterns that are related to high-order functions. In the same context, we will also take a closer look at the map method.

The first pattern is Functor. We will see what it is and how it is useful in our day-to-day programming. The second pattern is Monad. We have already seen some of it in the previous chapter. Here, we will look at it from the angle of higher order functions. Once the context is set, we will look at flatMap.

The third pattern is Monoid. We will see what it is and then look at foldLeft. We will apply what we have seen so far to an example in order to create an inverted index. Here, we will look at both the Java and Scala versions. We will again see how small, expressive, and succinct the Scala code is.

In the context of this example, we will look at the groupBy combinator and then again see an interesting application of foldLeft, while operating on Monoid.

We will wrap up with a discussion of the lazy collections. It is all pretty simple, dear reader. Don't let these big terms unnerve you. We will get it all. Get, set, go!

The strategy design pattern

The **strategy design pattern** encapsulates an algorithm and lets you choose the right one. It is really pretty simple. For example, going back to our family example, everyone loves to watch a movie over a weekend. However, dads love action flicks, moms love romantic movies, and kids being kids, love cartoons.

In Java, we would express the strategy pattern as follows:

```java
public interface MovieGenre {
  public String describeABit();
}


public class ActionFlick implements MovieGenre {

  @Override
  public String describeABit() {
    return "guns firing, fights, wild chases etc.";
  }

}
public class Animation implements MovieGenre {

  @Override
  public String describeABit() {
    return "cartoons! What else?";
  }

}

public class RomanticMovie implements MovieGenre {

  @Override
  public String describeABit() {
    return "some romantic flick";
  }

}
```

Here, our family members are input as a class:

```java
public abstract class FamilyMember {
  private final String name;
```

```
  private final MovieGenre movieGenre;

  public FamilyMember(String name, MovieGenre movieGenre) {
    super();
    this.name = name;
    this.movieGenre = movieGenre;
  }

  public String getName() {
    return name;
  }

  public MovieGenre getMovieGenre() {
    return movieGenre;
  }

  public void letUsGoForAMovie() { // 1
    System.out.println(getName() + " would love to watch " +
      movieGenre.describeABit()); // 2
  }
}

public class Dad extends FamilyMember {

  public Dad() {
    super("Dad", new ActionFlick());   // 3
  }

}

public class Mom extends FamilyMember {

  public Mom() {
    super("Mom", new RomanticMovie()); // 4
  }

}
public class Kid extends FamilyMember {

  public Kid() {
    super("Kid", new Animation());   // 5
  }

}
```

And finally, we express the driver class:

```
public class Driver {
  public static void main(String[] args) {
    FamilyMember[] allInTheFamily = new FamilyMember[] { new
      Dad(), new Mom(), new Kid() };

    for (FamilyMember familyMember : allInTheFamily) {
      familyMember.letUsGoForAMovie();
    }
  }
}
```

The salient points of this pattern are as follows:

- The `FamilyMember` class method, `letUsGoForAMovie()`, iterates all the family members and checks out what each member would like to watch
- It calls the `describeABit()` method on the `movieGenre` strategy
- As `Dad` loves action flicks, this is the movie genre strategy that is specified in the constructor
- And since `Mom` loves romantic movies, the strategy is defined accordingly
- Similarly, for `Kid`, we specify animation movies as the movie genre

A strategy in Scala land

By now you must have guessed that in Scala, things are far simpler. Let's try the following commands with creating an object:

```
object MovieStrategy extends App {

  type MoviePref = () => String // 1

  abstract class FamilyMember {
    def name: String
    def moviePref: MoviePref
  }

  case class Mom(name: String, moviePref: MoviePref) extends
    FamilyMember
  case class Dad(name: String, moviePref: MoviePref) extends
```

```scala
    FamilyMember
  case class Kid(name: String, moviePref: MoviePref) extends
    FamilyMember


  def letUsGoForAMovie[T <: FamilyMember](familyMember: T) = { // 2
    val mp = s"${familyMember.name} :  ${familyMember
      .moviePref() } "
    println(mp)
  }


  val mom = Mom("Mom", () => "some romantic flick") // 3
  val dad = Dad("Dad", () => "Action! Guns! Chase")
  val kid = Kid("Kid", () => "Animation for me")


  letUsGoForAMovie(mom) // 4
  letUsGoForAMovie(dad)
  letUsGoForAMovie(kid)
}
```

It is just a pageful.

The salient points of this strategy are as follows:

- We use a type definition to indicate the type of the strategy that we would accept. MoviePref describes a type of the function that takes no parameters and returns a String.

- The expression [T <: FamilyMember] is an **upper type bound** allows only the subtypes of the FamilyMember base type.

- The strategy algorithm is sent as constructor parameter, for the respective case class. The movieStrategy parameter is a function that takes no parameters and returns a String.

- We call the letUsGoForAMovie method and the specific strategy gets executed.

In this particular case, we could have just passed in a String. However, some moms may decide to go for an action flick on Fridays — so the strategy function could check the day of the week and act accordingly.

We are implementing the strategy by passing in functions. Functions are **first-class** objects in Scala (something is first class if it can be passed to functions, returned from functions, stored in variables, and so on. We can use it just like any other entities.)

Here are three underlying patterns that are related to higher order functions. Armed with the combinators know-how obtained in the previous chapter, we are now well poised to understand these patterns.

Functors

Let's say we have a function, X => Y. This function is transformed to another function List[X] => List[Y]. A higher order function that does this transformation is Functor, as shown in the following diagram:

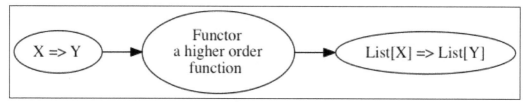

Figure 9.1: Functor translation

Here, we chose the List collection for ease of understanding. Instead of List, any collection will work (Refer to the next section for this):

```
object Functor extends App {

  def functor[X, Y](f: X => Y): List[X] => List[Y] = { // 1
    def fun : (List[X]) => List[Y] = (arg: List[X]) => arg match {
      case Nil => Nil
      case x :: xs => f(x) :: fun(xs)
    }
    fun
  }

  val p = List("Hi", "there")

  def doubleEachChar(s: String) = (for (c <- s) // 2
    yield c + "" + c).toList.mkString

  def numberOfLowerCaseChars(s: String) = s.filter(c => c.isLower).length
  // 3

  val f1 = functor(doubleEachChar) // 4
```

```
    val f2 = functor(numberOfLowerCaseChars) // 5

    println(f1(p)) // 6
    println(f2(p)) // 7
}
```

The salient points of the preceding code are as follows:

- Here, the higher order function, `functor`, is defined. It has two type parameters, `X` and `Y`. It takes as input, `f`, a function that converts `X` into `Y`. The `functor` **returns a function** that takes `List[X]`, invokes `f` on each element, and returns `List[Y]`.

- We have a function that takes an input string and doubles each character.

- We have another function that takes an input string and returns the number of lowercase characters in it.

- The `List[String] => List[String]` function is returned. Note that the `doubleEachChar` method is of the type `String => String`.

- The `List[String] => List[Int]` function is now returned. Note that the `numberOfLowerCaseChars` method is of the type `String => Int`.

- The `List(HHii, tthheerree)` list is now printed.

- After this, the `List(1, 5)` list is printed.

Maps

The map method takes a function as a parameter and applies it to each element in a container in order to return a new container. If the input container is `List`, the output container will be list too. If the input container is `Map`, the output container will be map too. If the input container is `Some`, the output container will also be `Some`. Remember that an option in Scala is a container too — holding one value — some — or holding nothing, that is, `None`).

Scala's `map` works like Functor, as shown in the following code:

```
scala> List(1, 2, 3) map { _ + 1 }
res0: List[Int] = List(2, 3, 4)
scala> Some(4) map { x => x+1 }
res1: Option[Int] = Some(5)
scala> Map(1 -> 2, 3 -> 4) map { z => (z._2, z._1) }
res2: scala.collection.immutable.Map[Int,Int] = Map(2 -> 1, 4 -> 3)
```

Something bugs you when you see them like this. The map method is defined in the traversable trait. How could map create the right type of container? The answer is using a builder, canBuildFrom. What does it build? It builds a builder.

You read right. This builds an appropriate builder for the type of input collection. So, for example, it builds Map for a map and List for a list:

```scala
import scala.collection.generic.CanBuildFrom
import scala.collection.mutable.ListBuffer


object MyMap extends App {
  def myMap[X, Y, Container[A] <: Traversable[A]](collection:
Container[X])(f: X ⇒ Y)(  // 1
    implicit builderSpec: CanBuildFrom[Container[Y], Y, Container[Y]]):
Container[Y] = {
    val buildIt = builderSpec()  // 2
    collection.foreach { x =>  // 3
      buildIt += f(x)   // 4
    }
    buildIt.result // 5
  }

  println(myMap(Seq(1,2)) { _ > 1 })
  println(myMap(List(1,2)) { _ < 1 })
  println(myMap(Vector(7, 8, 9)) { _ * 2 })
  println(myMap(ListBuffer(11, 12, 13)) { _ + 1 })
  println(myMap(Set(11, 12, 13)) { _ + 1 })
}
```

The salient points of the preceding code are as follows:

- We have the type parameters X and Y here. The method expects a function that takes a value of the type X and returns a value of the type Y. The method also takes a container that is traversable.

- We use the builder of builders in this case. Then, we in turn get a builder of the right type.

- The collection is a kind of traversable. Traversable is a trait that has the foreach method. As the collection objects, such as List, Vector, and Set are traversable, they use this method.

- We transform the input value, x, by passing it to the f function. The result of the transformation that is the return value of the function, is stored in the result collection.

- Finally, we return the accumulated result collection.

Monads

Let's say we have a function, X => List[Y]. This function is transformed to another function, List[X] => List[Y]. A higher order function that does this transformation is Monad.

Figure 9.2: Monad translation

Again, choosing the List container for ease of understanding, we go with the following commands:

```
object Monad extends App {
  def monad[X, Y](f: X => List[Y]): List[X] => List[Y] = {
    def fun : (List[X]) => List[Y] = (arg: List[X]) => arg match { // 1
      case Nil => Nil
      case x :: xs => f(x) ::: fun(xs) // 2
    }
    fun
  }
  def f1(n: Int) = (1 to n).toList // 3
  val f = monad(f1) // 4
  println(f(List(7,8,9)))  // 5
}
```

The salient points of the preceding code are as follows:

- We define a function, fun, that takes an argument, arg, of the type List[X].

- We iterate each element, x, of the input list. We invoke f(x) and get List[Y]. We **flatten** each list by concatenating the resulting lists together with the ::: operator.

- We have a function f1 that takes a number and creates a list of numbers.
- We create the monadic function into the variable f.
- The function f is invoked on an example list. Note that we get a flattened list as the output.

FlatMap

The flatMap method takes a function as a parameter, applies it to each element in a container, and flattens the overall result as shown in the following code:

```scala
scala> val f1 = (n: Int) => (1 to n).toList map { _ % 2 == 0 }
f1: Int => List[Boolean] = <function1>
scala> :t f1
Int => List[Boolean]
scala> List(2,3) flatMap f1
res4: List[Boolean] = List(false, true, false, true, false)
```

As earlier, f1 is of the type X => List[Y], where X is bound to Int and Y is bound to Boolean. Applying flatMap to List(2,3), which is List[Int], we get List[Boolean]. So, given the function, X => List[Y] we were able to get a transformation, List[Int] => List[Boolean].

Where does this come in useful? To know this, let's look at the following example:

```scala
scala> def f(x: Int) = if (x % 2 == 0) Some(x) else None
f: (x: Int)Option[Int]
```

The result of evaluating the function is Option, as shown in the following code. However, we wish to do something about this. Let's say, we add 1, if there is the Some value. If there is None, of course, there is no point adding 1 to nothing.

```scala
scala> f(10) match {
     |     case None => None
     |     case Some(x) => Some(x + 1)
     | }
res5: Option[Int] = Some(11)
```

Pattern matching does this. However, the following method is simpler as shown:

```scala
scala> f(10) flatMap (x => Some(x+1))
res6: Option[Int] = Some(11)
scala> f(11) flatMap (x => Some(x+1))
res7: Option[Int] = None
```

This looks succinct and simple. The preceding code roughly corresponds to the following Java code:

```
Integer x = f(11)
if (x != null) {
return x + 1;
}
```

In *Chapter 02, Singletons, Factories, and Builders,* we talked about singletons, Null Objects, and Scala's Options that are Null Objects.

In addition to being Null Objects, Options also encapsulate the application of a function based on the type of the argument, as Options come armed with map and flatMap:

```
def map[B](f: A => B): Option[B] =
  if (isEmpty) None else Some(f(this.get))
```

```
def flatMap[B](f: A => Option[B]): Option[B] =
  if (isEmpty) None else f(this.get)
```

The map applies the A => B input function to get Option[A] => Option[B]. The flatMap applies the A => Option[B] input function to get Option[A] => Option[B]. Like List, an Option is Monad.

Monoids

It is again pretty simple. From school math, we know that number multiplication is associative. And there is something like an identity element, 1 in case of multiplication. For example, the following expressions are equivalent:

```
(9*7)*2 = 9*(7*2)
```

Even if we do the multiplication in any order, we get back 126. The identity element now is 1. Concatenating strings is also associative. In the following code, the identity element is "". The "Singing" + "" string is the same as "" + "Singing", and the line contains multiple strings:

```
((("Singing" + " In") + " The") + " Rain")
```

This is the same as the one shown here:

```
("Singing" + " In") + (" The" + " Rain").
```

A data structure that obeys these rules is Monoid, and we have a natural way to use `foldLeft` in it, as shown in the following code:

```
scala> class MyMonoid {
     |    def iden = ""
     |    def f(x: String, y: String) = x.concat(y)
     | }
defined class MyMonoid
scala> val p = new MyMonoid
p: MyMonoid = MyMonoid@4e9658b5

scala> val list = List("Singing", " In", " The", " Rain")
list: List[String] = List(Singing In The Rain)
scala> list.foldLeft(p.iden)(p.f)
res1: String = Singing In The Rain
```

What is this big deal with being associative? It paves the way to parallelize operations. Though it does not make much sense in our singing in the rain example, for a collection that has thousands of entries, you could benefit from a parallel computation. Take a look at the following diagram as an example of Monoids:

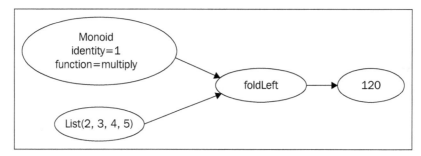

Figure 9.3: Monoids and foldLeft

What does all this buy for us programmers? Simple answer: simplicity of expression. Let's consider some illustrative examples to understand this.

An inverted index

I collect classic mystery novels, traditional British detective tales. These quaint, almost a century old puzzles have a soothing effect on me.

I do maintain a text file catalogue though (arrgh… no database for such a simple thing; a text file would do). The database I have is a csv file with the author surnames and then the book titles. Now, what if I want to reread a book again but can't remember its full name or the author name? In such a scenario, we would use an inverted index to find the complete name.

An inverted index is when you remember a word in the title and seem to look up the author's name. The following Java program prints the inverted index for a few of these books:

```java
class AuthorAndTitle {  // 1
  private final String authName;
  private final String title;

  public AuthorAndTitle(String authName, String title) {
    super();
    this.authName = authName;
    this.title = title;
  }

  public String getAuthName() {
    return authName;
  }

  public String getTitle() {
    return title;
  }
};
// imports elided - please see the source for the entire code
public class InvertedIndex {
  public static void main(final String[] args) {
```

```
final List<AuthorAndTitle> authorsToTitles = new
   ArrayList<>(); // 2


authorsToTitles.add(new AuthorAndTitle("Carr",
   "And So To Murder"));

authorsToTitles.add(new AuthorAndTitle("Carr",
   "The Arabian Nights Murder"));

authorsToTitles.add(new AuthorAndTitle("Christie",
   "The Murder Of Roger Ackroyd"));

authorsToTitles.add(new AuthorAndTitle("Christie",
   "The Sittaford Mystery"));

authorsToTitles.add(new AuthorAndTitle("Carr",
   "The Mad Hatter Mystery"));

authorsToTitles.add(new AuthorAndTitle("Carr",
   "The Plague Court Murders"));


Set<String> ignoreWordsSet = new HashSet<>(); // 3
ignoreWordsSet.add("To");

ignoreWordsSet.add("The");

ignoreWordsSet.add("And");

ignoreWordsSet.add("So");

ignoreWordsSet.add("Of");


final Map<String, List<String>> invertedIdx = new HashMap<>();
for (final AuthorAndTitle aTot: authorsToTitles) { // 4
  final String title = aTot.getTitle();
  final String[] words = title.split("\\W"); // 5


  for (final String w: words) {
    if (ignoreWordsSet.contains(w)) { // 6
      continue; // skip the word
      }
    if (!invertedIdx.containsKey(w)) { // 7
      invertedIdx.put(w, new ArrayList<String>());
      }
    final List<String> authNameList = invertedIdx.get(w);
```

```
        final String authName = aTot.getAuthName();
        authNameList.add(authName);
        }
    }


    for (Map.Entry<String, List<String>> e:
    invertedIdx.entrySet()) { // 8
    System.out.println(e.getKey() + " -> " + e.getValue());
    }}
}
```

The salient points of the preceding code are as follows:

- We have a class that represents a book's author and title.

- We also have the input list.

- We don't want to put common words such as The, Of, and For in the index. These are far too common and don't tell us anything valuable. We maintain a Set<String> type of these words.

- The actual algorithm for generating the inverted index, begins here.

- We split the title into words and iterate them.

- While iterating, if any of the words are marked to be ignored (that is, they are in ignoreWordsSet), we skip them.

- We initialize the list for the word if this is the first time we are seeing the word.

- We print the inverted index.

Quite a lot, isn't it?

Pipes and filters

Unix and Linux shells approach problems with the use of the pipes and filters pattern. Here is how we could implement the inverted index in GNU awk, gawk:

```
BEGIN {
  FS = "->"
}
{
  split($2, a, " ")
  for (x in a) {
    w = a[x]
```

```
        # print w
        iidx[w] = iidx[w] $1
    }
}
END {
    for(w in iidx) {
        print w " -> " iidx[w]
    }
}
```

Here is an example of pipes and filters:

```
echo 'Carr -> And So To Murder

Carr -> The Arabian Nights Murder

Carr -> The Mad Hatter Mystery

Christie -> The Murder Of Roger Ackroyd

Christie -> The Sittaford Mystery

Carr -> The Plague Court Murders' | sed -E 's/The|Of|And|To|So//g' | gawk
-f iidx.awk
```

Note that we pipe in the input text to sed. Sed filters out uninteresting words and passes on the rest of the text to awk. Awk generates the inverted index using features such as field splitting and associative arrays (which are similar to hash maps).

Note that I can combine these tools in many ways. For example, I could implement the logic of ignoring common words in the awk script itself. However, the use of the sed filter simplifies my awk script, which is a big gain.

The pipe line effectively iterates the input lines. However, the loops are implicit. Hence, both Awk and Sed iterate the input lines, do a bit of work, and pass on the intermediate result down the pipe line. This is an incredibly powerful mechanism.

Refer to http://martinfowler.com/articles/collection-pipeline/ to learn how prevalent this pattern is in programming.

Also, you can refer to http://www.tuxradar.com/content/exploring-filters-and-pipes and https://en.wikipedia.org/wiki/Pipeline_(Unix) for more information on the pipes and filters pattern.

Pipes and filters – the Scala version

Here is the Scala version. The for comprehension is similar in spirit to the preceding Unix shell pipe line:

```scala
object InvertedIdx extends App {
  val m = List("Carr" -> "And So To Murder",
        "Carr" -> "The Arabian Nights Murder",
        "Carr" -> "The Mad Hatter Mystery",
        "Christie" -> "The Murder Of Roger Ackroyd",
        "Christie" -> "The Sittaford Mystery",
        "Carr" -> "The Plague Court Murders") // 1
  val ignoreWordsSet = Set("To", "The", "And", "So", "Of") // 2
  val invertedIdx = (for { // 3
    (k, v) <- m // 4
    w <- v.split("\\W") // 5
    if !ignoreWordsSet.contains(w) // 6
  }
    yield(w -> k)).groupBy(_._1).map { case (k,v) => (k,v.map(_._2))} //
7
  println(invertedIdx)
}
```

The code is simple. We just write the code for comprehension, and the rest of it is so simple that it mostly works the first time you write it. If you ignore the setup of the input data, the code is effectively a five liner!

The salient points of the preceding code are as follows:

- In the preceding code, we set up the input data, where each author and title are a pair
- We set the words that are to be ignored
- The `for` comprehension computes the inverted index
- The pair is exploded into a key, k, and a value, v
- Each value, which is the book title string, is split on white space. The resulting words are iterated by the variable w
- We skip the word, w, if it is to be ignored
- Then, we go ahead to index the word that is paired with the author name

The `groupBy` combinator regroups the pairs by their first elements. Here is an example to better understand this:

```scala
scala> val list = List("x" -> "y", "z" -> "c", "x" -> "p")
list: List[(String, String)] = List((x,y), (z,c), (x,p))
scala> list.groupBy(_._1)
res0: scala.collection.immutable.Map[String,List[(String, String)]] =
Map(z -> List((z,c)), x -> List((x,y), (x,p)))
```

So, all the pairs with the x key are grouped under the key x.

We map the grouped map so that the repeated first element is eliminated, just leaving us with the second. Here is an illustration, applying to the preceding list:

```scala
scala> Map("x" -> List(("x","y"), ("x", "z"))).map { case (k,v) => (k,v.
map(_._2)) }
res5: scala.collection.immutable.Map[String,List[String]] = Map(x ->
List(y, z))
```

This may seem pretty dense at first; however, separating out and playing with the parts of the code will help you understand it better.

It is a Monoid

Hark back a bit dear reader. If you recall, we had said that a Monoid needs to be associative and should have an identity value.

Instead of using `groupBy` and friends, we can instead think of the collections as monoids and use `foldLeft`. Here is an example of how we do this:

```scala
scala> val list = List("x" -> "y", "z" -> "c",
"x" -> "p", "z" -> "d") // 1
list: List[(String, String)] = List((x,y), (z,c), (x,p), (z,d))
scala> Map[String, List[String]]() // 2
acc: scala.collection.immutable.Map[String,List[String]] = Map()
scala> list.foldLeft(acc) { (a, b) =>
     |    a + (b._1 -> (b._2 :: a.getOrElse(b._1, Nil)))
     | } // 3
res0: scala.collection.immutable.Map[String,List[String]] = Map(x ->
List(p, y), z -> List(d, c))
```

The salient points of the preceding code are as follows:

- Here, we have an input list of pairs that we need to convert into a map.
- As the identity value, we have an empty `HashMap` function.
- We use the `foldLeft` accumulator in the preceding `HashMap` method. For each key, if we don't have an entry as yet, we start with Nil. Otherwise, we take the already existing value, which is `List`. We add on the value to `List` that effectively grows by `1`.

Here is a diagram that clarifies this:

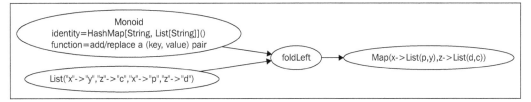

Figure 9.4: Converting a list of pairs to a map

So, using this idiom, we can write our inverted index code as shown in the following code:

```scala
scala> (for ((k, v) <- m; w <- v.split("\\W"); if !ignoreWordsSet.
contains(w) )
     |    yield(w -> k)).foldLeft(Map[String, List[String]]()) { (a, b) =>
     |    a + (b._1 -> (b._2 :: a.getOrElse(b._1, Nil)))
     | }
```

Now, replace the code, run it, and make sure that the outputs tally.

Lazy collections

All these combinators chaining are lovely, but there is a problem. For very large input data structures, this ends up creating intermediate copies.

Let's look at this aspect closely; you'll find that the solution is pretty revealing. Here is the Java code, just to set the stage:

```java
public class LargeLists {
  public static void main(final String[] args) {
    final int take = 5;
    for (int i = 1000, n = 0; i < 1000000 && n < take; ++i) {
      final int j = i + 1;
      final int k = j * 2;
      if (k % 4 != 0) {
        System.out.println(k);
        ++n;
      }
    }
  }
}
```

Here, we iterate a range of numbers from 1000 to 1000000. And for each number, we add 1 and then multiply the result by 2. If the result is divisible by 4, we discard it. Otherwise, we print the first five numbers from the result.

For example:

```scala
scala> val list = (1000 to 1000000).toList

scala> list.map(_ + 1).map(_ * 2).filter(_ % 4 != 0).take(5)

res0: List[Int] = List(2002, 2006, 2010, 2014, 2018)
```

The problem here is that every combinator creates an intermediate list. The Java code on the other hand, just does enough. Could we retain this spirit of immutability and still do enough? In other words, could we have the best of both worlds?

The way out is to use lazy collections. Let's have a look at the pictorial representation first, and then at the code.

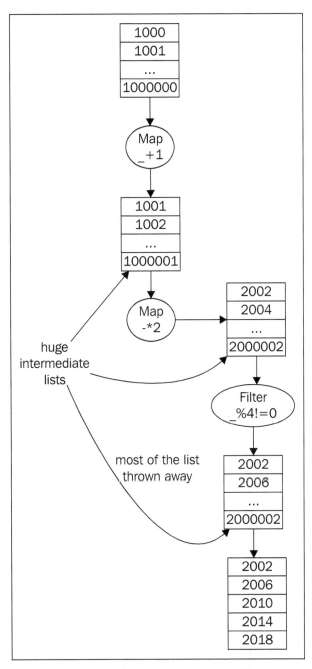

Figure 9.5: A big list processed immutably

Here the code operates on a list view:

```scala
object LazyLists extends App {

  def addOne(x: Int) = {
    println(s"addOne(${x}))" )
    x + 1
  }

  def multByTwo(x: Int) = {
    println(s"multByTwo(${x}))" )
    x * 2
  }

  def weedOutDivisibleByFour(x: Int) = {
    println(s"weedOutDivisibleByFour(${x}))" )
    x % 4 != 0
  }

  val list = (1000 to 1000000).toList.view // 1

  list.map(addOne).map(multByTwo).filter(weedOutDivisibleByFour).
  take(5).foreach { println }
}
```

The only change is at code labeled 1. We are operating on a list view. This evaluates the list in a lazy manner. The mapping of the addOne function is noted and remembered and the view is passed on. Next, the mapping of multByTwo and the filtering using weedOutDivisibleByFour is just remembered. Note that as yet, taking off elements from the collection is not **absolutely** required.

However, when we start printing, the evaluation cannot be delayed anymore. Then, all the mapping and filtering executables, and the resulting elements are printed one by one.

Note that this is the usual lazy list processing that we saw in *Chapter 04, Lazy Sequences – being lazy, being good*, and there is nothing magical about it.

If you run the program and look at the trace statements, you will see that this version works like its Java counterpart, as shown in the following code:

```
addOne(1000))
multByTwo(1001))
weedOutDivisibleByFour(2002))
2002
addOne(1001))
multByTwo(1002))
weedOutDivisibleByFour(2004))
```

The number `1000` is given to `addOne()`, and the result is passed to `multByTwo`. The result, `2002`, is then passed to the filtering function, `weedOutDivisibleByFour`. As `2002` is not divisible by `4`, it is the output.

Here, no intermediate lists were created. Instead, lists start on a number, processes it, and either prints or skips it. Only then does it start with the next number.

Summary

In this chapter, we looked at higher order functions, namely functions that take other functions as parameters, return a function as a result, or both.

We looked at the strategy pattern's Java implementation. We used Scala's higher order functions instead, to implement the algorithm encapsulation. Instead of Java classes implementing an interface, we passed in function literals. Then, we looked at three important patterns related to higher order functions.

We looked at Functors and then at the collection's map method. The second pattern was a Monad. We also looked at the `flatMap` method. The third pattern was monoids. In a related context, we also looked at `foldLeft`.

We applied the know-how to write an inverted index program. We looked at both the Java and Scala versions. The Scala code was short and idiomatic. We discussed the `groupBy` method and related idioms. Then, we used the `foldLeft` method instead of `groupBy` and saw how it works on a Monoid.

We wrapped up with a discussion on the lazy collections, and how they help us with just enough computation. In the upcoming chapter, we will look at what message-driven concurrency is, and actors. On to it!

10
Actors and Message Passing

"All the world's a stage, and all the men and women merely players: they have their exits and their entrances; and one man in his time plays many parts, his acts being seven ages."

- William Shakespeare

Consider a simple, almost everyday use case—going to the market and buying vegetables. Do we know who grew the produce? Do we know which patch of land gave us this leafy food? We usually don't know about this.

On the other side of the coin, does the farmer who grew the crop and took such loving care of it know who bought his produce ultimately? He does not. He is content enough in knowing that his produce goes to the market.

This is essentially decoupling. The producer does know that there is a consumer somewhere (otherwise, why would he produce in the first place?). The consumer, on the other hand, knows that the produce needs to be sown in the field first. This definitely happens somewhere. However, the consumer is not interested in the details.

The other startling aspect of this nature of transaction is that the number of producers and consumers is also unpredictable. As long as there is a place in the market for the produce to be kept, it really does not matter how many people take to farming and start producing food. It is always great that we have consumers for the food produced—the more the better!

Producers themselves are consumers of other things. A farmer is a consumer of fertilizers, and the factory is the producer.

In software, too, this strategy of producers not knowing about consumers and vice versa is used prominently. Hence , in this chapter, we will look at the Unix philosophy where we can connect producers and consumers together in the pipeline.

We will look at an example for this, a recursive grep. This will search a directory for files that have .txt extensions. In each file, it will search for a pattern.

The Unix pipeline solution is discussed to see how two processes work together and in parallel. This is an example of the producer consumer pattern. We will take a look at the pattern itself. The traditional Java solution of using threads comes next. We will implement the solution using the master slave pattern. We will also see the concept of a poison pill for orderly thread shutdown.

Next, we will discuss the event-driven way of things. Instead of polling for an interesting event, the idea is to register a callback that is fired when the event takes place. Immutability is golden when we try to design robust concurrent systems. Here, we will look at the leaky abstractions problem and the traditional solution. Finally, we will introduce Akka actors and present an actor-based solution for the problem. We will look at the advantages of the actors paradigm over threads.

So, here comes the Unix pipeline solution.

The recursive grep

Using the egrep program, we can recursively search a directory for a certain pattern. Here is a command line that is used to search a directory recursively for text files that contain a pattern:

```
~> find ./data -name '*.txt' -type f -print | xargs egrep 'this' /dev/
null
./data/a/a.txt:this is
./data/a/b/b.txt:this is file
./data/a/b/c/c.txt:this is file
```

Before we start grokking the command line, let's see what the xargs argument does. Xargs takes the egrep command, in this case, and invokes it with the arguments that it reads from the standard input.

For example, the following command searches for the pattern with help of the argument:

```
~> echo 'data.txt' | xargs egrep 'this'
```

The `xargs` argument invokes `egrep` on the `data.txt` file and searches for the `this` pattern. `Xargs` packs in as many arguments as possible (there is a limit) to minimize the number of `egrep` invocations. Refer to '*man xargs*' for more information.

Going back to our command, which has two parts:

- The `find` command recurs in the current directory. It matches files that satisfy a certain **criteria**. The criteria in this case is that the filename should have the extension `.txt`. Also, it should be a regular file as opposed to a directory named `laugh.txt`.

- The previous action prints the names of the files found in the standard output. These names are taken up by the `egrep` utility, and the files are searched for the `'this'` pattern in this case. In case the `find` command finds only one file that qualifies its criteria, `egrep` will work on only one file. In that case, `egrep` won't print the filename prefix; it thinks that you are searching for the file itself, so you already know about it. Egrep has no way of knowing that **it is executed as a part of the pipeline**. To fool it, we tack on `/dev/null`, which works as an empty file, and `egrep` will never find anything there.

There is an elaborate framework at work here. In case we are dealing with a huge directory, and `find` produces output too fast (fast producer) and the pipe fills up, the producer is blocked till the consumer has a chance to consume.

This scheme **decouples** `find` (producer) from the `egrep` (the consumer). The `find` command does not know that it is talking to anything like `egrep`. On the other hand, the consumer, `egrep`, does not know that it is getting the data from `find`.

Note that the programming language in which the `find` and `egrep` are written does not matter at all. Both these are written in C for performance reasons, however, the tool could be implemented in any language. We could write a tool in any language as long as it reads from standard input, transforms the line in some way, and writes to the standard output. A line is a string that is terminated by a new line. The line is the basic unit of work.

We can connect these tools together in any number of ways. In case we don"t have something ready, we could always write a **filter** of our own. If the filter abides by certain simple rules (such as reading from a standard input as mentioned earlier), it can be a part of the pipeline. Take a look at the following figure of a shell pipeline:

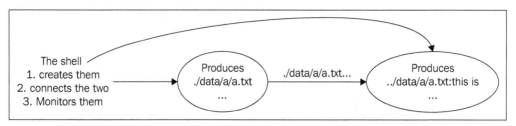

Figure 10.1: The shell pipeline

Another big theme is that a tool should *do one thing and do it well*. The Find command does the job of finding files, and it is quite powerful in what it does, for example, selecting files based on their types and name patterns use man find to refer to the manual page of the find command, for more information). The egrep command does text search, both case sensitive and case insensitive searches, and matches lines against regular expressions.

This is again the **single responsibility principle** (**SRP**) at work. This designs tools in such a way that they are highly cohesive. The advantage for this can be readily seen. Here, instead of searching for those files, I could instead inspect them one by one.

For example, the following command gives the output with the vim editor:

```
find ./data -name ''*.txt'' -type f -print | xargs -o vim
```

We have reused the find command and combined its results with the vim editor.

The producer/consumer pattern

This decoupling of the find command from the egrep command is intentional. Consumer not knowing about producers and vice versa has the following advantages:

- If we use a real message broker, such as the RabbitMQ server, we can even have producers and consumers written in different programming languages. For example, we can have a producer in Java and a consumer in Python. For the Unix example too, we can write filters in different languages and connect them together.

- We can have any number of producers and consumers.

- If some producers or consumers fail, the system keeps operating, although less effectively.

The last point is what makes us integrate different existing systems together. This is a very powerful concept.

Brokers offer many other conveniences too, such as storing, forwarding, and reliably delivering messages. Message brokers support patterns like point-to-point messaging or publish/subscribe. Refer to `https://www.rabbitmq.com/getstarted.html` for more information. The crisp examples at this link explain the concept via code snippets that you can play with. Take a look at the pictorial representation of this concept first:

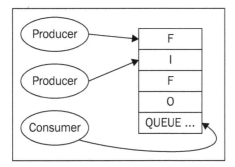

Figure 10.2: Producer/consumers and the FIFO queue

The consumer keeps waiting for the unit of work at one end of the pipe. The producers keep pushing the work units at the other end. This pipe can be realized by a **First In First Out (FIFO)** queue, which is a data structure that guarantees the first produced, first consumed order.

Refer to `https://www.cs.cmu.edu/~adamchik/15-121/lectures/Stacks%20 and%20Queues/Stacks%20and%20Queues.html` for a nice description of how FIFO queues work.

Now, let's look at an example in Java that uses all the preceding concepts that were outlined to perform the recursive grep program on a directory.

Threads – masters and slaves

One more concept at play here is of masters and slaves (also known as workers). The master spawns off a bunch of workers that are connected via a queue.

Then, a worker thread recurs in the directory. Once it finds a file with a `.txt` extension, it hands over the file to the egrep worker thread, as shown in the following figure. The egrep worker searches for the pattern in the file and prints out the matching lines:

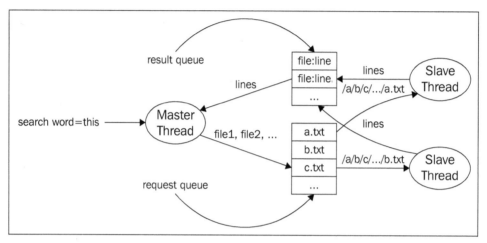

Figure 10.3: Master/slave threads

The master thread recursively traverses the directory, looking for files with the `.txt` extension. Here is an example of the Java code. We've used the excellent Apache `commons io` library for the file operations.

Here is how the Java code looks:

```
public class FilesFinder extends DirectoryWalker
    implements Runnable { // 1

    private final String directory;
    private final BlockingQueue<File> inputQueue; // 2

    public FilesFinder(final String directory, final
        BlockingQueue<File> inputQueue) {
        this.directory = directory;
```

```
    this.inputQueue = inputQueue;
  }

  @Override
  protected void handleFile(final File file, final int depth,
    final Collection results) throws IOException { // 3
  try {
    inputQueue.put(file);
    } catch (final InterruptedException e) {
      e.printStackTrace();
    }
  }

  public void run() {
    final File startDir = new File(directory);
    try {
      walk(startDir, null); // 4
      } catch (final IOException e) {
      e.printStackTrace();
    }
  }

}
```

The salient points of the preceding code are as follows:

- In the preceding code, we saw that the `FilesFinder` class finds the files. It extends `DirectoryWalker` from Apache's `commons io` library.

- The `inputQueue` is of type `java.util.concurrent.BlockingQueue`, which is shared by both the producer and the consumer. Producer(s) pushes a unit of work (a file here) on this queue so that some consumer(s) can work on the file. In our case, this consumer is the `GrepAFile` class.

- For each file found, the `handleFile` callback is invoked. The file is passed in as an argument so that we can **visit** the file. In this example, our visit amounts to pushing the file on the queue.

- After this, the directory walk takes place.

Here is the code that is used to search for patterns in the file:

```
// import elided
public class GrepAFile implements Runnable { // 1
  private final String pat;
```

```
    private final BlockingQueue<File> inputQueue;

    public GrepAFile(final String pat, final BlockingQueue<File>
      inputQueue) {
      super();
      this.pat = pat;
      this.inputQueue = inputQueue;
    }

    public void run() {
      while(true) {
        try {
        final File file = inputQueue.take(); // 2
        if (itsAPoisonPill(file)) { // 3
          return;
        }
        final List<String> lines = FileUtils.readLines(file,
          ""UTF-8"");
        for (final String line: lines) { // 4
        if (line.contains(pat)) {
          System.out.println(file.getName() + "" : "" + line);
          }
        }
        } catch (final InterruptedException e) {
      e.printStackTrace();
      } catch (final IOException e) {
      e.printStackTrace();
      }
    }
    }

    private boolean itsAPoisonPill(final File file) { // 5
      return file.getName().equals(""last.txt"");
    }

}
```

The salient points of the preceding code are as follows:

- This is the consumer of files. It searches for the pattern in the file and prints the matching lines on the console.

- The unit of work, `File`, is picked up from the queue. If there is no work available, the call gets blocked.

- The **poison pill** is a way to tell the thread to stop what it is doing and die. It is a pretty melodramatic name. This needs to be the last item to be used. In our case, we just go by the filename `last.txt`. This works well for us to illustrate the concept.

- The work of searching the file for the pattern takes place here. We also print the matching files on the console.

- The poison pill is then defined.

Here is the driver code:

```
public class GrepRecursive {
  private final String pattern;
  private final String directory;
  private final BlockingQueue<File> requestQueue;

  public GrepRecursive(final String pattern, final String
    directory) {
    super();
    this.pattern = pattern;
    this.directory = directory;
    this.requestQueue = new LinkedBlockingDeque<File>();

  }

  private void grep() throws InterruptedException {
    final FilesFinder ff = new FilesFinder(directory,
      requestQueue); // 1
    final GrepAFile gaf = new GrepAFile(pattern,
      requestQueue); // 2

    final Thread producer = new Thread(ff);
    final Thread consumer = new Thread(gaf);

    consumer.start();
    producer.start();

    producer.join();
    consumer.join(); // 3
    }
  public static void main(final String[] args) throws
    InterruptedException {
    final GrepRecursive qr = new GrepRecursive(""this"",
      ""../../code/data"");
    gr.grep(); // 4
  }

}
```

Finally, we have the driver that creates the workers and kicks off things.

The salient points for preceding code are as follows:

- It creates a `File Finder` worker
- It creates the `grep` worker
- It starts both and then waits for them to finish
- Then, we call the `grep()` method after setting up the pattern and the root directory

Events

We all use keyboards in our everyday work life. We use them to write code and compose e-mails. There is no knowing when a certain key will be pressed. However, when a key is pressed, the user expects certain action to happen—for example, the letter indicated by the key should appear in the editor when we are writing code.

This seems natural enough, doesn't it? However, note that there is an elaborate mechanism at work here. The operating system piece needs to know which key was pressed. So, one way to find this out is to go and ask periodically whether any key was pressed, and if so, which one. This is called "**polling**" for any interesting information. When we poll, we go and ask the driver, at intervals about any status regarding whether a key was pressed or not, as shown in the following figure:

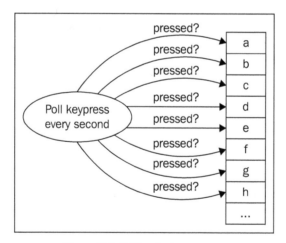

Figure 10.4: Polling for key presses

This polling approach is problematic for the following reasons:

- We really don't know whether the polling interval of a second is enough
- In case someone is not using a keyboard for an hour or more, we would end up wasting precious computing cycles just checking for possible key presses

Instead of using this approach, we should model the key presses as events and the operating system piece as an **observer**. The moment a key is pressed, an event takes place. This event is sent across to the interested parties who have expressed an interest (the observers).

Refer to `https://sourcemaking.com/design_patterns/observer` for more information on observers. Here, we are essentially observing and **reacting** to an external stimulus. Take a look at the following figure where the key presses are modeled as events:

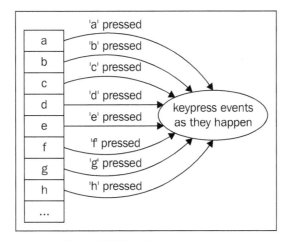

Figure 10.5. Reacting to key presses

Immutability is golden

Time and again, we have talked of making data structures immutable. We can pass them around without two threads changing the shared state (that is, data structure) at the same time. Immutability makes up for less moving parts, and hence the reasoning about such systems is simpler.

The issue here is when two (or more) threads update a shared object, a **race condition** is said to happen. Refer to `http://stackoverflow.com/questions/34510/what-is-a-race-condition` to know more about races.

If we make the objects immutable, race conditions are not possible, as no thread can update it.

To make a mutable instance immutable, we could wrap it up. However, we should not leak any references out. Here is an example Java snippet that illustrates this problem:

```java
public class Wrapper {
  private final List<Integer> value;

  public Wrapper() {
    value = new ArrayList<Integer>();
    //...
  }

  public List<Integer> getValue() {
    return value;
  }

  public synchronized void someAlgorithm() {
    // mutate the list
  }
}
```

We have created an abstraction all right. However, this is a leaky abstraction. Take a look at `http://simpleprogrammer.com/2013/10/14/leaky-abstractions-holding-us-back/` for a great explanation of leaky abstractions.

Someone could set the value using the reference obtained via the getter. This problem gets exacerbated as IDEs like Eclipse allow you to generate getters and setters. Though in this case, Eclipse would be smart enough to generate a getter only, as the getter itself leaks out the list reference.

Note that if we could somehow make sure that the list itself is unmodifiable, it would solve the problem. The solution is to expose a **read-only view** of the collection. If we write the getter as follows, the problem is solved:

```
public List<Integer> getValue() {
  return unmodifiableList(value);
}
```

This version is better for two reasons:

- It is easier to reason about race conditions—only the thread holding the object lock (meaning in a synchronized method) can change the list.

- It is easier to guarantee class invariants. Note that, here, we have marked the `value` field as `private`. We want to control the updates made to it, as it is really an internal state. The outside world is welcome to read it (for example, print it to a console).

Wouldn't it have been better if the default list were immutable? In that case, we could expose it directly and not need to wrap it up. Moreover, Someone could set the mutate the list reference obtained via the getter. Adding setters willy-nilly would exacerbate the problem.

You got it right, this is what Scala does. The `List` class is immutable now.

The threading example has its shares of problems though. Here are some of them:

- What if the `egrep` worker thread fails for some reason? We will have to code in order to restart it.

- What if we fail to account for some shared state update? Unknowingly, someone may leak a mutable reference or use an unsafe API.

- There is an inherent limit of how many threads we can create. Umm—around 4,096 threads for 1 GB of memory. This could be severely limiting as our load grows.

- Failing to lock correctly can give us the dreaded heisenbugs. It is very hard or, at times, impractical to debug race condition bugs. Refer to `http://swreflections.blogspot.in/2012/08/fixing-bugs-that-cant-be-reproduced.html` for more information on concurrency heisenbugs.

However, there is a much better way to do this. Please welcome in Actors and Akka!

Akka actors take the stage

Akka is a Scala library, which let's us implement the message-based concurrency systems. An actor is like a small program with a message queue of its own. You can only get an actor to do some work by passing it a message.

Here is our `FileFinder` object as an actor:

```
import akka.actor._
import akka.util.Timeout
import scala.io.Source

object FileFinder { // 1
  def props() = Props(new FileFinder)
  case class FileFinderMsg(pat: String, rootDir: String)
}


class FileFinder extends Actor { // 2
  import FileFinder._
  import context._
  import java.io.File

  val grepActor = system.actorOf(Props(new GrepAFile), ""GrepAFile"") // 3

  def recurseIntoDir(dir: File): Iterable[File] = { // 4
    val itsChildren = new Iterable[File] {
      def iterator = if (dir.isDirectory) dir.listFiles.iterator else Iterator.empty
    }
    Seq(dir) ++: itsChildren.flatMap(recurseIntoDir(_))
  }

  def receive = { // 5
    case FileFinderMsg(pat, rootDir) => {
      val d = new File(rootDir)
      for(f <- recurseIntoDir(d) if f.getName.endsWith("".txt"")) {
```

```
    import GrepAFile.GrepMsg


    grepActor ! GrepMsg(pat, f)  // 6
  }
}
case _ => self ! PoisonPill  // 7
  }
}
}
```

The salient points of the preceding code are as follows:

- In the preceding code, we saw that the `FileFinder` object is a companion object. It defines the `FileFinderMsg` class that the actor handles.

- After this, the `FileFinder` object becomes an actor. It can receive messages and does useful work.

- `GrepActor`, which is a child actor, is created after this.

- The method, `recurseIntoDir`, recursively traverses a directory tree, and searches for qualifying files.

- After the actor message loop for each file is found (with the extension `.txt`), the grep actor is given the pattern and the file.

- The `!` send operator is used to send a message to another actor. More specifically, we **tell** the actor to do something. This is the "fire-and-forget" way of passing a message to another actor. The message is sent asynchronously, and the control returns immediately.

- The message loop is exhaustive. If we get any other type of message, the actor is fed a poison pill and the actor dies as a result.

Here is the Java code where `grepFile` becomes an actor:

```
import java.io.File

import akka.actor.{ Actor, Props, PoisonPill }

import scala.io.Source

object GrepAFile {
  def props() = Props(new GrepAFile)
  case class GrepMsg(pat: String, file: File)
}

class GrepAFile extends Actor { // 1
```

```
import GrepAFile._

def receive = { // 2
  case GrepMsg(pat, file) => { // 3
    for (line <- Source.fromFile(file).getLines()) {
      if (line.contains(pat)) {
        println(s""${file.getName} : ${line}"")
      }
    }
  }

  case _ => { // 4
    println(""GrepAFile exitting"")
    self ! PoisonPill
  }
}
}
```

The salient points of the preceding code are as follows:

- We saw that the GrepAFile object becomes an actor.
- The message loop—note again—is exhaustive.
- Upon receipt of the GrepMsg message, we get the unit of work to do stuff. We iterate the lines of the file and print the matching ones.
- If we receive any other message that the actor cannot deal with, the actors swallow a poison pill.

Here is the driver through which we put the actors to work:

```
import akka.actor.{ ActorSystem , Actor, Props }

object Main extends App {

  implicit val system = ActorSystem(""packt"") // 1

  val fileFinder = system.actorOf(Props(new FileFinder),
""FileFinder"")

  import FileFinder.FileFinderMsg

  fileFinder ! FileFinderMsg(""this"", ""../data"") // 2
}
```

The salient points of this example are as follows:

- In the preceding code, we saw that the top-level actor, `FileFinder`, is created using the `ActorSystem` variable

- Now, the ball starts rolling, and we send the pattern and the directory root to grep in

Advantages

- We did not set up any queues but just wrote simple Scala code, in particular, a message loop. There was no explicit locking, as there is no shared state
- The `FileFinder` actor communicated with the `GrepAFile` actor purely via message passing. It is very similar to how we distribute work among people. We can reason about the code easily. Both the actors are executed in parallel. Also, we could have a `GrepFile` actor per file, as actors are not costly

Summary

We had a whirlwind tour of concurrency mechanisms. It started with the producer/consumer pipeline of Unix. Then we saw the inherent principles behind the pipeline, namely decoupling and each tool doing at least one thing. This is the essential Unix philosophy.

We looked at the recursive grep worker as an example. After the pipeline solution, we looked at the producer/consumer implementation in Java. We looked at the problems of performing multithreading by ourselves. We also saw how we need to take extreme care not to introduce race conditions.

Races can take place when there is a possibility of the same state getting updated by multiple threads. We saw one example of a leaky abstraction and how immutability helps us gain the ground back.

Keeping in mind the perils of multithreading, we looked at Akka, Scala's popular actor library. We implemented the solution using Akka actors and saw the simplicity of the messge driven concurrency paradigms.

With all this know-how under our belt, let's look at the paradigm shift that all these new techniques have brought about.

11
It's a Paradigm Shift

We have come a long way, dear reader, having dabbled with many Scala features. Hopefully, it was an exciting and fruitful journey. All along, we witnessed a novel approach to the programming process. Scala provides startlingly unconventional ways to help us become more effective. Ultimately, we have witnessed a fundamental change in approach, a paradigm shift.

What we need to do remains mostly the same, though. The idea is to cut down the boilerplate and write code at a higher level of abstraction, for example, the need to pass around bits of code, as a comparator to sort things. We will see how the functional way makes sorting a snappy affair.

Java code is pretty verbose when we compare it with Scala. Functions play an important part in being expressive and succinct.

Error handling has always been a tedious chore. Scala's Try (yes that is a capital T) helps us handle errors in a functional way.

Futures and Promises come after that. These are tools to write asynchronous code. These tools are very different from Java threads and allow us to work at a higher level of abstraction.

Domain-Specific Languages (DSLs) are extremely useful tools. We wrap up with a look at Scala's Parser combinators and how easily we can parse text.

Let's ring the curtain up for the grand finale!

Verbosity

The imperative way of things is pretty verbose. Here is a case in point. The filtering and flattening is pretty long:

```java
import java.util.List;

public class Books {
  private final String author;
  private final List<String> titles;

  public Books(String author, List<String> titles) {
    super();
    this.author = author;
    this.titles = titles;
  }

  public String getAuthor() {
    return author;
  }

  public List<String> getTitles() {
    return titles;
  }
}
------------------ PickUpInterestingStuff.java ----------------

import java.util.List;

import com.google.common.collect.Lists;

public class PickUpInterestingStuff {
  public static void main(String[] args) {
    List<Books> listOfBooks = Lists.newArrayList();
    listOfBooks.add(new Books("Carr", Lists.newArrayList("The Mad
Hatter Mystery",
      "The Blind Barber")));
    listOfBooks.add(new Books("Christie",
      Lists.newArrayList("Death On The Nile",
        "Murder in Mesopotamia")));

    // pre Java 8
```

```
    List<String> titlesFor = Lists.newArrayList();

    for(Books books: listOfBooks) {
      if (books.getAuthor().equals("Carr")) {
        titlesFor.addAll(books.getTitles());
      }
    }
    System.out.println(titlesFor);
    // if using Java 8
    listOfBooks.stream().filter(book -> book.getAuthor().
  equals("Carr")).forEach(b -> System.out.println(b.getTitles()));
    }
  }
```

If we use Java Version 8, the code is more succinct and shorter. Here is the Scala version:

```
case class Books(author: String, titles: List[String])
val list = List(Books("Carr", List("The Mad Hatter Mystery",
  "The Blind Barber")), Books("Christie", List("Death On The Nile",
  "Murder in Mesopotamia")))
list.filter(_.author == "Carr").flatMap(_.titles).foreach { println }
```

This is much better! Note also that you cannot change the Books attribute once the object is created. Both the list and its elements cannot be modified.

The number of bugs go down as there are less moving parts! A big reason for this succinctness is we can so easily pass around bits of code, aka functions. In Java, we need to extend an interface and that is some code. In C, we can pass around functions (function pointers), but we don't have much type safety.

Sorting it out!

Scala provides `sorted`, `sortBy` and `sortWith` methods. We will take a quick look at them and then tackle an interesting memoization problem.

Sorted

The sorted method uses **natural ordering** amongst the elements of the collection. Natural ordering well, seems natural.

For example, given the following numbers:

1, 11, 22, 2

The natural ordering would be:

1, 2, 11, 22

And the alphanumeric ordering would be:

1, 11, 2, 22

Alternatively, please see http://blog.codinghorror.com/sorting-for-humans-natural-sort-order/ for more on natural ordering.

Here is sorted in action:

```scala
scala> import scala.util.Random
import scala.util.Random
scala> val list = List.fill(10)(Random.nextInt(100))
list: List[Int] = List(5, 49, 37, 56, 54, 64, 9, 85, 76, 28)
scala> list.sorted

res0: List[Int] = List(5, 9, 28, 37, 49, 54, 56, 64, 76, 85)
```

This, of course, creates a new list as the original list is immutable.

SortBy

This method sorts on an attribute of the compound type. For example, given a list of tuples:

```scala
scala> val l = List((2,3), (1,9), (4,7))
l: List[(Int, Int)] = List((2,3), (1,9), (4,7))

scala> l sortBy (_._1)
res0: List[(Int, Int)] = List((1,9), (2,3), (4,7))

scala> l sortBy (_._2)
res1: List[(Int, Int)] = List((2,3), (4,7), (1,9))
```

Or given a list of objects, you can sort by any attribute of the object:

```
scala> case class Record(num: Int, str: String)

scala> val list = List(Record(9, "zeroth"), Record(4, "first"),
Record(11, "second"), Record(3, "third"), Record(22, "fourth"))

list: List[Record] = List(Record(9,zeroth), Record(4,first),
Record(11,second), Record(3,third), Record(22,fourth))

scala> list.sortBy(r => r.num)

res0: List[Record] = List(Record(3,third), Record(4,first),
Record(9,zeroth), Record(11,second), Record(22,fourth))
```

This sorts the objects by its num attribute. It is short as most of the boilerplate is eliminated.

What if we want to sort in descending order? Well, you can always resort to comparators and sort with them.

SortWith

This version allows us to pass a function to be used as a comparator. Note how succinct and expressive the code is:

```
scala> list.sortWith { (first, second) =>
     |      first.num > second.num
     | }

res2: List[Record] = List(Record(22,fourth), Record(11,second),
Record(9,zeroth), Record(4,first), Record(3,third))
```

Comparing it with the Java sort, see how simple it is when we use functions.

Scalaish Schwartzian transform

The Perl language has a fantastic memoization idiom, the Schwartzian transform. When we are sorting a list of objects, the sorting efficiency is improved. This is a generalized algorithm, though.

Here is the problem. Given a list of pairs of strings:

```
scala> val list = List(("one", "First"), ("two", "Second"), ("three",
"third"))
```

We wish to sort the list:

- In lexicographical ordering by the first entry and in case of a tie by the second entry
- In lexicographical ordering by the second entry and in case of a tie by the first entry
- Just by the length of the first entry
- By the string length of the first entry and in case of a tie by the second entry

We could do any of these by passing in the comparison criteria as a function.

For example, by sorting the list by the length of the second element:

```
scala> list.sortWith(_._2.length < _._2.length)
res4: List[(String, String)] = List((one,First), (three,third),
(two,Second))
```

The problem is the length of the strings is computed again and again. When we are sorting a collection of objects with a complex sort criteria involving many fields, this becomes a concern.

Run the following snippet and see how many times the length of the same string gets computed:

```
scala> case class Name(firstName: String, lastName: String)
defined class Name


scala> def cmp(first: Name, second: Name) = {
     |      println(s"Computing length of <${first.firstName}>")
     |      val len1 = first.firstName.length
     |      println(s"Computing length of <${second.firstName}>")
     |      val len2 = second.firstName.length
     |
     |      len1 < len2
     | }
cmp: (first: Name, second: Name)Boolean


scala> val list = List(Name("one", "First"), Name("two", "Second"),
Name("three", "third"))
```

```
list: List[Name] = List(Name(one,First), Name(two,Second),
Name(three,third))
```

```
scala> list.sortWith(cmp)

Computing length of <two>

Computing length of <one>

Computing length of <one>

Computing length of <two>

Computing length of <three>

Computing length of <two>

Computing length of <two>

Computing length of <three>
```

The output shows we are wasting CPU cycles and recomputing string lengths. Could we somehow compute the string length and cache it?

The Schwarzian transform is an elegant solution to this problem. It memoizes the intermediate computation that is, cahces the results thereby avoiding the redundant scalls.

Before we look at the algorithm, we need to know a bit more about sorting pairs:

```
scala> val list = List(
     |      ("Reggie Tennyson", 1),
     |      ("Mabel Spence", 3),
     |      ("Monty Bodkin", 12),
     |      ("Albert Peacemarch", 2)
     | )
scala> list.sorted
res1: List[(String, Int)] = List((Albert Peacemarch,2), (Mabel Spence,3),
(Monty Bodkin,12), (Reggie Tennyson,1))
```

 Whoa! I could sort by pairs if the individual pieces forming it were ordered. (Refer to http://www.scala-lang.org/api/2.11.2/index.html#scala.math.Ordered for more information).

Given all of the preceding, let's piece together the transform algorithm:

```scala
scala> def nameLens(name: Name) = (name.firstName.length, name.lastName.length)

nameLens: (name: Name)(Int, Int)
```

It is just a method — converting the Name object to a tuple, each element of which is the length of the first and last names.

This is the list we need to sort:

```scala
scala> val list = List(Name("Always the", "First"), Name("A second", "Helping"), Name("A thumping", "third"))
```

Mapping the nameLens function over the list gives the following output:

```scala
scala> list map nameLens

res1: List[(Int, Int)] = List((10,5), (8,7), (10,5))
```

We applied the function to the input list. Note that we have precomputed the lengths (that is, we have cached the lengths of the strings):

```scala
scala> list map nameLens zip list

res2: List[((Int, Int), Name)] = List(((10,5),Name(Always the,First)), ((8,7),Name(A second,Helping)), ((10,5),Name(A thumping,third)))
```

We zipped the list of name lengths with the input list. It is a new list with the name lengths clubbed with the input Name element:

```scala
scala> list map nameLens zip list sortWith {
     |     (x, y) =>
     |        x._1._1 < y._1._1
     | }
res3: List[((Int, Int), Name)] = List(((8,7),Name(A second,Helping)), ((10,5),Name(Always the,First)), ((10,5),Name(A thumping,third)))
```

We sort the list, and the criteria now works on the precomputed cached length data. Retrieving the interesting part is simple now; we just go and pull it out with a map:

```scala
scala> list map nameLens zip list sortWith {
     |     (x, y) =>
     |        x._1._1 < y._1._1
     | } map (_._2)
res2: List[Name] = List(Name(A second,Helping), Name(Always the,First), Name(A thumping,third))
```

Here is a figure illustrating the flow:

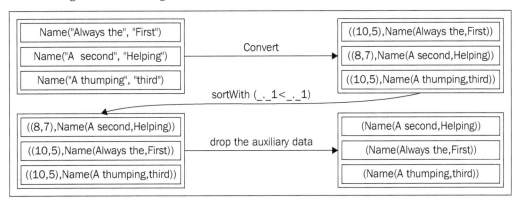

Figure 11.1: Sorting the list

We have tacked on the precomputed lengths as a tuple. As the tuples are **ordered** (that is, we can use < and > to compare elements of a tuple), we sort using it.

We have seen this principle in action before. We are caching the lengths of the fields, so we avoid computing them again and again. You guessed it right—this is memorization in action.

Functional error handling

Handling errors is one tricky aspect of writing code. Error handling is the essential devil we simply can't do without.

The procedural world relies on returning error codes from functions, suffering from the same problem because of null checks. We could possibly miss checking. Also, the actual business logic gets lost in the tangled error handling code.

A case in point is file handling. Opening files and reading the contents, for example, could result in exceptions. As another example, the file may not exist (perhaps there is a typo in the filename), or it may not have requisite permissions.

Throwing an exception is a much better idea. The calling code cannot ignore it, at the very least it has to catch the exception.

You can, off course, use Java style try/catch blocks in Scala. As the try/catch block is an expression, you can assign its value to a variable:

```
scala> case class HandsUp(msg: String) extends Exception(msg)
defined class HandsUp

scala> def warnThem = throw HandsUp("Hands Up!!!")
warnThem: Nothing

scala> val p = try {
     |    warnThem
     | } catch {
     |    case HandsUp(msg) => msg
     | }
p: String = Hands Up!!!
```

However, there is a more functional way. Here is a snippet that checks if a file's contents are the same when read backwards (that is, if the file content is a palindrome):

```
import java.io.{FileNotFoundException, File}
import scala.util.{Failure, Success, Try}
import scala.io.Source._

object PalindromeFiles extends App {
  def checkFileExt(f: File, ext: String) = Try { // 1
    if (f.getName.endsWith(ext))
      f
    else
      throw new RuntimeException("Wrong extension")
  }
  def fileIsPalindrome(f: File) = Try { // 2
    val lines = fromFile(f).mkString.stripLineEnd
    if (lines == lines.reverse)
      f
    else
      throw new RuntimeException("Not a palindrome")
  }
  def checkFileIfItIsAPalindrome(f: File) = checkFileExt(f, ".txt").
flatMap(fileIsPalindrome(_))
```

```
  val checkOne = checkFileIfItIsAPalindrome(
    new File("./two.txt")) // 3
  val checkTwo = checkFileIfItIsAPalindrome(
    new File("./abrakakarba.txt")) // 4
  val checkThree = checkFileIfItIsAPalindrome(
      new File("./fileDoesNotExist.txt")) // 5
  checkOne.foreach(println)
  checkTwo.foreach(println)
}
```

The salient points for the preceding code are as follows:

- We check for the file extension. If it is something other than what we need, we throw an exception.

- We read all contents of the text file as a string, minus the last newline character, if any. We reverse the string check in order for the strings to be palindromes of each other. If the check fails, we again throw another exception.

- The pipelining of checks is run on `two.txt`, which is not a palindrome. Again, the file name is not printed.

- A successful pipeline occurs when the file name is printed.

- We try the pipeline on a file that simply does not exist–the pipeline keeps silent. The file name is not printed.

Try is very much like Scala's Option. Did you notice the absence of any try/catch code? When the pipeline is in error, the combinators following it simply don't touch it. but instead pass it on. Only when it gets a `Success(File)` does the real work happen.

Note that in the event any combinator receives a failure, it does nothing but just pushes the failure on to the next one in line. The overall effect is if there is an exception anywhere, the rest of the pipeline simply does nothing!

Here comes a flow chart depicting the flow:

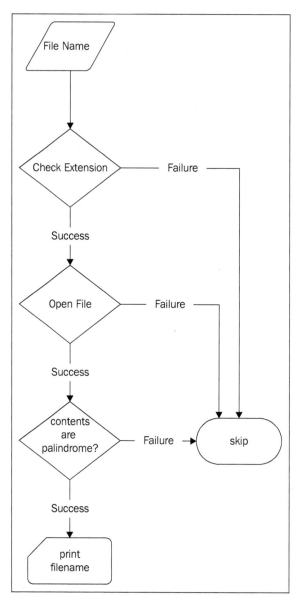

Figure 11.2: Error handling flowchart

Pattern matching

If you want to check out the exact error, then you can pattern match the `Try`. Change the code as shown:

```
def printResult(x: Try[File]) = x match {
  case Success(f) => println(f) // 1
  case Failure(e) => println(e) // 2
}


printResult(checkOne)
printResult(checkTwo)
    printResult(checkThree)
```

This prints the error messages. At code labeled as 1, we print the filename and at code labeled as 2, we print the error message. At 2, the variable `e` is the exception caught by the `Try`.

Threads and futures

You can use threads in Scala, however, there is a better way. You can use threads the same way in Scala, too, but there are alternative approaches. It is yet one other important paradigm shift.

We have seen an example of message-driven concurrency using actors and the Akka framework.

Here is a contrived example, which sums up a list of numbers. The code forks a thread to compute the summation, simulates a delay, and returns the answer to the main thread:

```
--------ListSumTask.java--------
import java.util.List;
import java.util.concurrent.TimeUnit;

public class ListSumTask implements Runnable {

  private final List<Integer> list;
  private volatile int acc; // 1

  public ListSumTask(List<Integer> list) {
    super();
    this.list = list;
    this.acc = 0;
```

```
    }

  public void run() {
    sleepFor(4);
    for (Integer i : list) {
      acc += i;
    }
  }
  private void sleepFor(long secs) {
    try {
      TimeUnit.SECONDS.sleep(secs);
    } catch (InterruptedException e) {
      // TODO Auto-generated catch block
      e.printStackTrace();
    }
  }

  public int getAcc() {
    return acc;
  }
}
--------TaskDriver.java--------
import java.util.Arrays;
import java.util.List;

public class TaskDriver {
    public static void main(String[] args) throws InterruptedException
{
        List<Integer> list1 = Arrays.asList(10, 11, 12, 13);
        List<Integer> list2 = Arrays.asList(14, 15, 16);

        ListSumTask task1 = new ListSumTask(list1); // 2
        Thread t1 = new Thread(task1);
        ListSumTask task2 = new ListSumTask(list2); // 3
        Thread t2 = new Thread(task2);

        t1.start();
        t2.start();
        t1.join();
        t2.join();

        int total = task1.getAcc() + task2.getAcc();
        System.out.println("Total sum = " + total);
    }
}
```

Most of this code should not pose any problem for you. However, there are a couple of things to be aware of.

The following are the salient points foe the preceding code are as follows:

- Note the accumulator variable `acc` in the thread class. We need to mark this as volatile so when the parent thread reads it, correct memory visibility is enforced.
- A task is necessary to process the first list. This sums up the list, and the delay is simulated via the sleep method.
- Another task on the same line is needed to process the second list.

A computation is synchronous or asynchronous. When we invoke a method, we wait until its execution is complete. This is the sequential flow model we intuitively think of while writing code. However, consider sending a piece of mail via the application.

We usually cannot block the calling thread, waiting for the mail delivery to complete. The rest of the system could get starved (the thread is blocked instead of doing some useful work), so we instead follow the asynchronous model.

A good example is a telephone call versus sending a letter by surface mail. We wait for the call to get connected with the other party and follow the synchronous way. On the other hand, we do not wait for the letter to reach the intended party at the sent address. This would be highly wasteful.

Scala's Futures

We have seen Akka, actors, and the message-driven concurrency model. However, actors are long-running objects, resilient with the monitoring and supervision built in.

With this being said, at times, we will need something simpler, without all the power and setup complexity, and still be able to do asynchronous computation.

Scala Futures is the answer. Note that these are way ahead of Java's Futures (`java. util.concurrent.Future`). Using Java's Futures, we can either block or need to poll it frequently, and that becomes a pretty awkward computing model.

So, with a bit of all that under our belt, here we go:

```scala
import scala.concurrent.{ExecutionContext, Future, Promise, Await}
import scala.concurrent.duration._
import ExecutionContext.Implicits.global

object Futures extends App {
  def from(n: Int): Stream[Int] = { // 1
    Thread.sleep(2000)
    n #:: from(n + 1)
  }

  val printNumbers = Future { // 2
    val start = from(10).take(4)
    start.foldLeft(0) { _ + _ }
  }

  val f = printNumbers map { // 3
    case 46 => {
      println("Got it")
    }
    case _ => println("Huh?")
  }


  Await.ready(f, 60 seconds) // 4
}
```

The following are the salient points for the preceding code are as follows:

- We simulate a long-running activity via Scala streams. The thread sleeps for 2 seconds and then returns the next number.
- We collect the result 10, 11, 12, 13. We take four elements from the stream, sum them up, and return the result. This creates a future.
- We create a new future by applying a function to the successful result. You can also use flatMap if the computation on one future depends on the result of another.
- We wait 60 seconds for the future to complete. Note the literal 60 seconds method invocation. Please see the information box for more on why this works.

The syntax 60 seconds is the same as 60.seconds(); however, Scala allows dots and parents to be omitted. Now, we are invoking a method, seconds() on 60 which is an Int. The Int variable does not have any seconds() method. The compiler searches for an implicit conversion that takes an Int and returns something that has the missing method defined.

As the code imports DurationInt, the expression is rewritten as DurationInt(60).seconds(). This is the implicit conversions magic we have seen earlier.

Please refer to https://github.com/scala/scala/blob/v2.11.5/src/library/scala/concurrent/duration/package.scala#L1 for more information.

Parser combinators

Parsers are everywhere. A Scala program text needs to be parsed first for it to run. We parse a JSON to get at the data structure. We then try to make sense of the text and pull out something useful from it.

Parsing may succeed or fail. For example, the text may not have what we are looking for. It may have something else equally interesting. At times, we'll want to retry different parsers on a piece of text, hoping that one of them might succeed.

A parser looking for a number in the string how do you do? will fail as there is no number. However, a parser looking for greetings will succeed.

The idea behind Scala's Parser combinators is to compose more complex parsers from simpler ones. We compose parsers that can be tried one after another or one instead of another.

Here is a simple example of parsing a double from a string:

```scala
scala> :paste  // 1
// Entering paste mode (ctrl-D to finish)
import scala.util.parsing.combinator._  // 2
object ParseANumber extends RegexParsers {  // 3
  def number: Parser[Double] = """\d+[.]?\d*""".r ^^ { _.toDouble }  // 4
}
^D (control-d) here...
```

The regular expression is followed by a function. The operator ^^ says that if the pattern is recognized, then apply the following function.

Here is a sample run of the preceding parser:

```
scala> ParseANumber.parse(ParseANumber.number, "9.3445")
res12: ParseANumber.ParseResult[Double] = [1.7] parsed: 9.3445

scala> ParseANumber.parse(ParseANumber.number, "9.")
res13: ParseANumber.ParseResult[Double] = [1.3] parsed: 9.0

scala> ParseANumber.parse(ParseANumber.number, "9")
res14: ParseANumber.ParseResult[Double] = [1.2] parsed: 9.0
```

This parser parses a double from an input string.

The salient points for the preceding code are as follows:

- You need to paste code into the Scala REPL. The `:paste` command starts the paste mode. You break out of the paste mode back to the REPL command prompt by pressing *Ctrl + D*.
- We import the parsing machinery.
- We extend a `RegexParser`. Regular expressions are a basis for our parsing. There is also a `JavaTokenParser`, which provides convenient methods like `ident` to parse Java identifiers.
- We define a method number, which is a small parser itself. It parses a double from an input string.

The parser is exercised on example input and illustrates how the parser works for different input strings.

Here is more fun, as we try parsing a sequence of words, in order:

```
scala> :paste
// Entering paste mode (ctrl-D to finish)

import scala.util.parsing.combinator._

object ParseHowDoYouDo extends RegexParsers {
  def sequence1 = "how" ~ "do" ~ "you" ~ "do"  // 1
  def sequence2 = ("how" | "do") ~ ("you" | "do") ^^ {  // 2
    case t => println(t)
  }
}
// Ctrl-D here...
```

The salient points for the preceding code are as follows:

- The ~ is a parser combinator. It combines the parsers; each parser is a literal string. There is an implicit conversion from `java.lang.String` to `Parser[String]`. These string literal parsers match just themselves. When all these parsers are combined, we get a parser that parses "how do you do?" The input `howdoyoudo` my friend also works.

- This is another little complex parser made by combining smaller parsers. In addition to the ~ combinator, it uses the | combinator. If the parser cannot find `how`, it gives another try to see if `do` matches. The `^^` is used to marry a function to the parser, which is invoked if the parsing is successful:

```
scala> ParseHowDoYouDo.parse(ParseHowDoYouDo.sequence1, "how do "
+

     |    "you do my friend")

res0: ParseHowDoYouDo.ParseResult[ParseHowDoYouDo.~[ParseHowDoYo
uDo.~[ParseHowDoYouDo.~[String,String],String],String]] = [1.14]
parsed: (((how~do)~you)~do)


scala> ParseHowDoYouDo.parse(ParseHowDoYouDo.sequence2, "do " +

     |    "do my friend")

(do~do)

res1: ParseHowDoYouDo.ParseResult[Unit] = [1.6] parsed: ()
```

Here is a slightly complex parser, which takes a string of numbers and an operator. The parser runs the operator on the list and returns the result:

```
import scala.util.parsing.combinator._


class Calcy extends RegexParsers {

  def add(x: Int, y: Int) = x + y

  def mul(x: Int, y: Int) = x * y

  def num: Parser[Int] = """(0|[1-9]\d*)""".r ^^ { // 1
    _.toInt
```

```scala
  }

  def numList: Parser[List[Int]] = rep(num) // 2

  def op: Parser[(Int, Int) => Int] = ("+" | "*") ^^ { // 3
    case "+" => add _
    case "*" => mul _
  }

  def expr: Parser[Int] = (numList ~ op) ^^ { // 4
    case t => {
      val list = t._1 // 5
      val f = t._2
      list.reduceLeft((x,y) => f(x,y)) // 6
    }
  }
}
object TestCalcy extends Calcy {
  def tryParsing(s: String) = {
    parse(expr, s)
  }
}

object AnAssignmentParser extends App {
  println(TestCalcy.tryParsing("1 2 3 4 +")) // Outputs 10
  println(TestCalcy.tryParsing("1 2 3 4 *")) // Outputs 24
}
```

The salient points for the preceding code are as follows:

- This is a simple number parser. We try to pull out a numeric string and invoke toInt() on it.

- The rep method repeatedly uses the given parser to parse the input. The num parser is used repeatedly to pick up as many numbers as it can.

- The `op` parser parses an operator, either an addition operator (`+`) or a multiplication operator (`*`). We return a function of type `(Int, Int) => Int` when we see an operator.

- The `expr` parser is the final parser we have. It combines the `numList` and `op` parsers and expects the operator to follow the list of numbers.

- The function, associated with the `expr` parser, destructures the parsers and gets the list of numbers and the operator function.

- We reduce the list of numbers by applying the function.

Note that we have just expressed the grammar and what should happen when the parsing is successful. We have not written much of anything else. All the boilerplate of the actual parsing process is hidden from us. For example, if one parser fails, another is applied (if there is any).

Summary

Paradigm shift is a fundamentally alternate approach to program design. It invites us to think in radically different ways. Sorting, parsing, error handling, and concurrency have very different forms in Scala compared to Java.

Scala provides some stock sorting methods. We took a look at them and then came up against a problem of needless computation when sorting objects. The solution is the Schwartzian transform, a memorization technique. This is a Perl idiom, however, the idea is pretty general. We saw its Scala implementation.

Error handling is usually messy. The scheme of returning error codes always has the risk of us forgetting to check for errors. Exceptions are an improvement. Scala provides a nice solution so the error handling blends into the computation pipeline. We looked at the Try/Success/Failure family with an example.

We can use threads; however, Scala provides Futures and Promises. These are much easier to use when performing asynchronous computations. We can approach concurrency in a much more functional way. Futures are pretty handy for pipelining.

Parsing texts is a very common programming activity. Scala's parser combinators provide the framework so one can compose complex parses out of simpler ones. We have seen higher order parsers being composed from smaller parsers.

So, hopefully you have, by now, gotten a sense of the paradigm shift. The best way is to apply what we have learned and experience the paradigm shift firsthand.

Happy learning!

Index

O

Object Relational Mapping (ORM) 76
observer
  about 237
  URL 237
Open/Closed principle (OCP) 22
Option class
  reference link 33
  using 33, 34
overloaded constructors
  using 48, 49

P

parser combinators 261-265
partial functions
  about 167, 168
  visitor pattern 169, 170
partially applied function 138
pattern guard 165
pattern matching
  about 55, 56, 161, 162
  deconstruction, with case statements 56-58
  de-structuring 163
  partial functions 167
  pattern guards 165
  stack overflows 58
  tuple explosion 165, 166
  typed patterns 164
patterns
  about 19
  command design pattern 20
  strategy design pattern 21
persistent data structures 53, 70, 72
pipes
  implementing 217, 218
  implementing, in Scala 219, 220
  reference link 218
poison pill 235
polling 236
producer/consumer pattern 230, 231
proxy pattern
  URL 76
  using 76-78
proxy server 76

Q

queues
  URL 231

R

RabbitMQ
  URL 231
race condition
  URL 238
READ/EVALUATE/PRINT LOOP (REPL) 1
read-only view, of collection
  URL 239
recursion
  about 53
  forms 73
recursive case 55
recursive grep 228-230
recursive streams 83, 84
recursive structures 53-55
reduce combinator 197-201
refactoring
  reference link 133
  URL 84, 118
referential transparency 8-10
Replace Conditional with Polymorphism
    refactoring
  URL 157
Resource Acquisition Is
    Initialization (RAII)
  about 142
  reference link 142
rich interfaces, Scala 108-110

S

Scala
  about 1
  rich interfaces 108-110
  stackable modifications 114
  streams 81
scalaidioms 18, 19
Scalaish Schwartzian transform 249-253
Scala way
  iterating by 182, 183
Scalaz
  URL 18

Thank you for buying
Scala Functional Programming Patterns

About Packt Publishing

Packt, pronounced 'packed', published its first book, *Mastering phpMyAdmin for Effective MySQL Management*, in April 2004, and subsequently continued to specialize in publishing highly focused books on specific technologies and solutions.

Our books and publications share the experiences of your fellow IT professionals in adapting and customizing today's systems, applications, and frameworks. Our solution-based books give you the knowledge and power to customize the software and technologies you're using to get the job done. Packt books are more specific and less general than the IT books you have seen in the past. Our unique business model allows us to bring you more focused information, giving you more of what you need to know, and less of what you don't.

Packt is a modern yet unique publishing company that focuses on producing quality, cutting-edge books for communities of developers, administrators, and newbies alike. For more information, please visit our website at www.packtpub.com.

About Packt Open Source

In 2010, Packt launched two new brands, Packt Open Source and Packt Enterprise, in order to continue its focus on specialization. This book is part of the Packt Open Source brand, home to books published on software built around open source licenses, and offering information to anybody from advanced developers to budding web designers. The Open Source brand also runs Packt's Open Source Royalty Scheme, by which Packt gives a royalty to each open source project about whose software a book is sold.

Writing for Packt

We welcome all inquiries from people who are interested in authoring. Book proposals should be sent to author@packtpub.com. If your book idea is still at an early stage and you would like to discuss it first before writing a formal book proposal, then please contact us; one of our commissioning editors will get in touch with you.

We're not just looking for published authors; if you have strong technical skills but no writing experience, our experienced editors can help you develop a writing career, or simply get some additional reward for your expertise.

Mastering Play Framework for Scala

ISBN: 978-1-78398-380-3   Paperback: 274 pages

Leverage the awesome features of Play Framework to build scalable, resilient, and responsive applications

1. Demystify the quandaries of web development using Play Framework.

2. Test and debug your apps by using Play's built in testing framework.

3. Master the core features of Scala through a comprehensive coverage of code and examples for different scenarios.

Scala for Java Developers

ISBN: 978-1-78328-363-7   Paperback: 282 pages

Build reactive, scalable applications and integrate Java code with the power of Scala

1. Learn the syntax interactively to smoothly transition to Scala by reusing your Java code.

2. Leverage the full power of modern web programming by building scalable and reactive applications.

3. Easy to follow instructions and real world examples to help you integrate java code and tackle big data challenges.

Please check **www.PacktPub.com** for information on our titles